Secrets
of
Esther

Donna K. Maltese

Secrets of Esther

*A Devotional
for Women*

BARBOUR
PUBLISHING

The Secrets of Esther

The book of Esther has everything you could hope for in a good story—good as well as evil, feasts as well as fasts. It has an orphan who becomes a heroine and queen, a villain who falls into traps he himself has set, a faithful surrogate father and follower of God, and a plethora of secondary characters who move the story along with their own subplots, providing even more excitement and intrigue.

But that's not all. Esther is one of only two Bible books (the other being the Song of Solomon) that does not contain the name of God. Yet even though His name is not mentioned, you can see His hand behind every action, His movement in every plot twist, and His providence in every outcome. He is the One who turns all evil plotted against His people into their ultimate good and very salvation.

The one who grows the most in this wonderful story is the young heroine Esther. Yet who would she be without her surrogate father, teacher, and adviser, Mordecai?

Most interesting of all, God provides us with a question to consider: For what reason have we come to God's kingdom and entered upon His stage for such a time as this?

Let us now enter into Esther's story and find our own place and purpose within this fascinating biblical account.

Note: The verses at the beginning of each devotion were written by J. B. Steele and appeared in his book *Sacred Poetical Paraphrases and Miscellaneous Poems* (New York: Hosford & Ketcham, 1863).

*And who knows but that
you have come to the kingdom
for such a time as this and
for this very occasion?*

ESTHER 4:14 AMPC

Always Hope

Ahasuerus sat on Persia's throne;
His royal crown with many jewels shone;
Each gem declared his wide extended sway;
A hundred seven-and-twenty states his laws obey.

As we enter into Esther's story, we're introduced to Ahasuerus (aka Xerxes), who "reigned from India to Ethiopia over 127 provinces" (Esther 1:1 AMPC). His riches, powers, and territories were vast.

Yet before we go further, we should understand why we're being told about this foreign king. After all, we want to hear about Esther, the orphan girl who became a queen. But to understand why and how she ended up in that position, we first must understand why she and her fellow Jews were scattered across King Ahasuerus's territory.

How did the people of God get to this place? God had vowed that the kingdom of David would endure forever (2 Samuel 7:16). So what happened? Did God renege on His promise? And if so, can we trust that any of His other promises will hold true?

To find answers to these questions, we look to the Word. There we find there was once one kingdom called Israel that was ruled first by David and later by his son Solomon. But because God's people abandoned Him and began bowing to other gods, after Solomon's death the kingdom was split into two separate kingdoms: Judah and Israel.

Afterward God repeatedly warned His people what would happen if they continued to bow to other gods, worship idols, follow the customs of pagan countries, and so on. He reminded them that

He would abandon them as they had abandoned Him. Yet they persisted to defy Him.

Thus, many kings and misdeeds later, Israel fell to and was taken into exile by Assyria (2 Kings 17:6–20). One hundred thirty-six years later, Judah fell too and was taken into captivity by Babylon. All this happened long before Esther's time. And now, the territory of those fallen kingdoms had been absorbed into the Persian Empire under King Ahasuerus. Thus, when Esther's story begins, we see it wasn't just *some* Jews who were under Ahasuerus's rule and scattered throughout his land but *all* Jews.

Although Israel had received no definite time period from God for their return to their homeland, Judah had. "You will be in Babylon for seventy years. But then I will come and do for you all the good things I have promised, and I will bring you home again" (Jeremiah 29:10 NLT).

What can we learn from this? That God's people, although they may be scattered, can rely on the promises of their Creator. This is why we have hope that no matter where we go, God can and will bring us home again.

"I know the plans I have for you. . . . They are plans
for good and not for disaster, to give you a future and a hope."
JEREMIAH 29:11 NLT

Lord, in You and Your plans I place my hope. Amen.

Pomp and Pride

From Ethiopia to the Indian strand,
Province on province bowed at his command;
His oriental standard, wide unfurled,
Waved o'er the proudest empire of the world.

What riches Ahasuerus's empire obtained! What pride he felt in displaying his wealth to others! For it was not just the lavish feasts he hosted to show off his affluence but the trappings surrounding him and his guests—the beautiful curtains and wall hangings, silver rings, marble pillars, and gold and silver couches, all of which "stood on a mosaic pavement of porphyry, marble, mother-of-pearl, and other costly stones" (Esther 1:6 NLT).

Imagine dining at such a sumptuous feast, drinking wine in gold goblets. There, free-flowing wine began to make your heart glad. But with that alcohol skewing your eyesight, your initial wonder at the opulence that surrounded you could easily morph into envy, causing you to covet what the king had and you lacked! After all, you might begin thinking, you took more risks than he during battles of war. Day after day you put your life on the line. And what did you get in return? A feast that at first seemed fantastical and generous. And then, after a few sips and some raucous talk, you start to wonder why you are not blessed with such riches. Is it just a matter of blood or class that earns the fortunes of this world? Are people like you always to be downtrodden and never to get ahead? Why is it that the rich seem to get richer, and the poor poorer? These are questions that are still being asked today!

Yet God would not have you thinking that way. For a slight to your pride, harbored and nurtured within, causes you to be ungrateful, forgetting all He has done for you (Deuteronomy 8:11–14). You become like Ahasuerus, who needed to keep accumulating more and more wealth to satisfy his ego.

Instead of falling into this swamp of dissatisfaction and discontent, before pride makes headway, pray to God for help, saying, "Give me neither poverty nor riches; feed me with the food that is needful for me, lest I be full and deny you and say, 'Who is the LORD?' or lest I be poor and steal and profane the name of my God" (Proverbs 30:8–9 ESV).

Don't allow pride to keep you from being happy for others when things are going well for them. Don't allow your inner refrains of *Why not me?* to drown out a spoken "Good for you!" to them. If you want to have true happiness, put away pride and be humble, for "God has had it with the proud, but takes delight in just plain people" (1 Peter 5:5 MSG).

> *First pride, then the crash—the bigger*
> *the ego, the harder the fall.*
> PROVERBS 16:18 MSG

Lord, help me to be grateful for and content
with what I have, to be honest and modest in Your
eyes as well as in the eyes of others. Amen.

Generous to a Fault

The times were genial. Ahasuerus calls
His honored nobles to his splendid halls.
From every province of his vast domain
The men of rank, of power, of influence came.

*A*hasuerus displayed the wealth of his vast kingdom by holding a six-month feast for all his officials and staff, the armies of Persia and Media, as well as nobles and governors of the provinces over which he reigned. Afterward, he hosted a seven-day banquet for all those living in the palace in Susa.

The wine flowed freely and many of the revelers at this all-male bash were told to drink as much as they wanted (Esther 1:7). However, when wine flows freely, things often go awry—not only for those who over-imbibe but for those around them.

We need only consider the righteous Noah (Genesis 7:1). God instructed him to build an ark so that he and his family alone would be saved from floodwaters that would soon overtake the earth. When the waters receded and Noah and his family disembarked, Noah planted a vineyard. Then one day he got drunk and passed out in his tent. Naked. His son Ham saw his nakedness and went out and told his two brothers. The latter covered their father's shame and vulnerability. Upon waking and being told what had happened, Noah must have felt like he'd looked: a fool. In response, he cursed Canaan, the son of Ham, and blessed his sons Shem and Japheth (Genesis 9:20–27).

Next was Lot. He, a recent widower, had escaped with his two daughters from Sodom, and the three of them were living alone in a mountain cave. Thinking they'd never know a man and that consequently their family line would be wiped out, the two daughters got their father drunk two nights in a row and, unbeknownst to him, slept with him! As a result of the daughters becoming pregnant by their father, the peoples known as the Moabites and Ammonites came into being (Genesis 19:30–38).

Lastly, we have Abigail's husband Nabal, whose name means "fool." He refused to extend kindness in return for services David had rendered. Sensing trouble, Abigail went out and made peace with David. When she arrived back home, her husband was very drunk. When he sobered up the next day, she told him what she'd done. Shocked, her husband had a heart attack and died (1 Samuel 25).

God doesn't prohibit the drinking of alcohol (Proverbs 31:6). But He does remind us that "wine is a mocker, strong drink a brawler, and whoever is led astray by it is not wise" (Proverbs 20:1 ESV). So, with our second look at King Ahasuerus, we can see that along with humility, wisdom is not one of his attributes, and his drinking will soon make him a brute.

> *Don't get drunk with wine, which leads to*
> *reckless actions, but be filled by the Spirit.*
> Ephesians 5:18 hcsb

> *Lord, give me wisdom, that I might*
> *overimbibe only with Your Spirit. Amen.*

The Honorable Decision

'Twas modesty, not duty, gave the word
Of disobedience to her rightful lord.
To duty's shrine we bow and give our praise,
But love the modesty that disobeys.

While in one area of the fortress the king and his men were imbibing unlimited alcohol, King Ahasuerus's queen, Vashti, was holding a banquet for the women of the palace.

On the seventh day of the feast, the prideful king, "high on the wine" and eager to show off his beautiful wife, "ordered the seven eunuchs who were his personal servants. . .to bring him Queen Vashti resplendent in her royal crown" (Esther 1:10–11 MSG). But she declined his drunken offer. She "refused to come, refused the summons delivered by the eunuchs" (Esther 1:12 MSG). And because she refused, the king burned with anger—especially because his queen's refusal was witnessed by so many others. All this gives credence to the warning in Proverbs 23:29–30: "Who has woe? Who has sorrow? Who has contentions? Who has complaining? *Who has wounds without cause?* Who has red eyes? Those who linger long over wine" (NASB, emphasis added).

Yet according to Persian customs, the queen had every right to refuse her king's command. For she, even more so than the wives of other men, was to be kept out of the public eye, to be secluded from view. Thus this order by her king, in Vashti's eyes, could, in accordance with the mores of the day, be dismissed. Regardless of her view of the matter, the king was now furious—more incensed than soused. About this scene and circumstance, F. B. Meyer writes,

*Whenever men are overcome with wine, there is
grave peril for women. Coarseness, indelicacy,
and impurity troop in at the door, which has been
unlocked by the excess of wine. Who can tell the
anguish which has been caused to women, children,
and the dumb creation through the intemperance
of man!**

Perhaps you've experienced similar circumstances at the hands
of an authority figure. That person, whether drunk or sober, may
have put you in a precarious position, between the proverbial rock
and a hard place, leaving you only one option in your own eyes and
God's. And that option was the honorable one: to deny the request,
regardless of the personal or professional cost to you.

That's a difficult decision to make at times. Yet it is the right
one. When you take that narrow road, that hard path, know that
God will stand by your side. He'll not only give you the courage, wisdom, strength, and power to face the consequences of your decision
but also help you endure them.

> *Whoever pursues righteousness and kindness
> will find life, righteousness, and honor.*
> PROVERBS 21:21 ESV

---

*When I'm placed in a precarious position, Lord, I look to You
to give me the courage to make the honorable decision and to
stand by my side as I endure the consequences. Amen.*

---

*F. B. Meyer, *Bible Commentary* (Wheaton, Illinois: Tyndale House Publishers,
Inc., 1979), 211.

Out of Control

The king before his nobles feels
The pangs of wounded pride, and he who wields
O'er Persia's realm an unresisted power,
Is roused to wrath in that wild frenzied hour.

When Queen Vashti refused her inebriated husband's command to join his merry party, Ahasuerus was one red-faced sovereign. It appears this man who led great armies and ruled a grand empire could master neither his drinking nor his wife! Anger and alcohol, ably feeding off each another, can easily lead a person down the wrong path. Feeling things spiraling out of control and upset that he wasn't getting his way, Ahasuerus overflowed with rage!

We've all been there but perhaps didn't recognize it in the moment, the anger welling up inside us when we can't have the things we dearly desire, when people don't do as we would like them to do, when we realize we are not masters of the universe.

It's a hard pill to swallow, yet it is reality. Perhaps it's especially hard for an earthly king, a person with vast wealth, to realize there may be something out of his control. But don't we consider ourselves queen of our own little universe, small as it may be? And don't we too suffer disappointment when the raise we want is not offered, the lover we desire does not love us in return, the child we gave birth to does not obey, or the once-amorous man we married becomes less affectionate over the years?

Fortunately, we believers have a God who continuously reminds us that we can leave all our needs and desires, disappointments and discouragements, pride and prejudices at His doorstep. We can fall back onto God and take solace in the fact that He is the only one who is truly in control (Romans 13:1–2). He is in charge of all the leaders, all the people, all the events, and all the circumstances we encounter.

What relief there is in that truth. It means we don't have to burden ourselves with nonstop efforts to get things right, with the stress that comes with trying to rule our world. Perhaps we can even smile when we realize our best-laid plans have come to nothing. For then we can remind ourselves that God has a greater plan. And His plan is for our good—nothing more, nothing less.

We are assured and know that [God being a partner
in their labor] all things work together and are [fitting
into a plan] for good to and for those who love God and
are called according to [His] design and purpose.
ROMANS 8:28 AMPC

How wonderful to know, Lord, that You are my partner in
this life and that every plan You come up with will be the right
one for me in the long run. In Jesus' name I pray, amen.

Counselors

The king is seated in his wounded pride;
His robed and jeweled princes by his side.
The sage Memucan, rising o'er the rest,
His counsel gave, his judgment. . .expressed.

King Ahasuerus, the ruler of a vast empire and commander of the two great armies of Persia and Media, couldn't even get his wife to obey him. Chagrined, and looking like a drunken fool before all those beneath him (for in his eyes, everyone was beneath him), Ahasuerus was enraged. What could he do but consult with those who were considered to have greater wisdom than he?

Thus, Ahasuerus conferred with seven men, experts in law and justice, and asked them, "What must be done to Queen Vashti? . . . What penalty does the law provide for a queen who refuses to obey the king's orders, properly sent through his eunuchs?" (Esther 1:15 NLT).

Memucan, one of King Ahasuerus's counselors, rose and spoke for all. He made the argument that the queen not only had wronged the *king* by her actions but had wronged everyone in the king's provinces. After all, when her actions became public, all wives would end up disobeying the orders of their husbands, resulting in rampant fits of anger and contempt of the wives for their husbands throughout the kingdom.

The only solution, said Memucan, was for King Ahasuerus to get rid of Vashti and find a new queen. By taking this course of action, "husbands everywhere, whatever their rank, will receive proper respect from their wives!" (Esther 1:20 NLT).

This plan was approved by the king and all his counselors.

Here we must pause and consider those whom Ahasuerus asked to give of their wisdom. Would such a king surround himself with counselors who were truly wise or with minions who would flatter his ego and support his every whim? Perhaps these so-called wise men were too drunk or too much the sycophants to protest Memucan's advice. Either way, Queen Vashti's doom was pronounced and agreed upon unanimously.

Powerful men have met with bad counselors before. King David's son Amnon, lusting for his sister Tamar, followed the bad advice of his friend and cousin Jonadab. He proceeded to rape his sister and then discard her, leading to her shame and his death (2 Samuel 13).

Then there was King David's former counselor Ahithophel, who sided with David's son Absalom when he attempted to usurp his father. Ahithophel eventually hanged himself and Absalom was killed while hanging from a tree (2 Samuel 15–18).

Fortunately, female followers of Jesus know the best counselor a woman could ever have: Father God (James 1:5). He is no flatterer or sycophant. He will give you only truth and wisdom, even if you are His royal offspring.

> *The LORD says, "I will guide you along the best pathway*
> *for your life. I will advise you and watch over you."*
> PSALM 32:8 NLT

To You alone I pray for wisdom, Lord.
Show me the right path. Amen.

The Man Behind the Curtain

A royal ordinance, that Vashti wear
No more the crown, or royal honors share.
And place the crown upon another's brow,
Disposed respect to yield and reverence show.

Upon the advice of counsel, King Ahasuerus "sent letters to all parts of the empire, to each province in its own script and language, proclaiming that every man should be the ruler of his own home and should say whatever he pleases" (Esther 1:22 NLT). He did this so that "husbands everywhere, whatever their rank, will receive proper respect from their wives!" (Esther 1:20 NLT).

In this new decree, we not only learn more about King Ahasuerus but uncover the first bit of irony in the book of Esther. For here was a man (a ruler of 127 provinces and commander of two armies) who couldn't even get his own wife to obey him. And here he was issuing a universal order—in each province's own script and language—that *all* women should honor their husbands! The second irony is that by sending out this decree to all in his land, Ahasuerus was ensuring that everyone in his kingdom—not just the people of Susa—would get wind of his marital problems. At the same time, we begin to see how God, although not mentioned by name, was moving behind the scenes to enable a young Jewish orphan to become the empire's queen.

This new inroad began with a king who was not only prideful but unable to rein in the amount of wine he drank. Intoxicated, he made a request of his queen, one that was beneath both of them. When this request was denied and his anger kindled (another loss of self-control), he listened to bad advice. This series of events reveals how pliable Ahasuerus is in the hands of others, as well as how rash he is in making judgments and pledging his royal seal.

Clearly we see that God was behind both Vashti's refusal to obey her husband's request and the advice given by the king's counselors that she be dethroned.

Yet we should not be surprised how easily God can use and maneuver humans—husbands and wives, believers and nonbelievers, even kings! As Proverbs 21:1–2 tells us, "The king's heart is in the hand of the Lord, as are the watercourses; He turns it whichever way He wills. Every way of a man is right in his own eyes, but the Lord weighs and tries the hearts" (AMPC).

We have a God who works not only behind the scenes but through all people for the good of His children.

Clearly, you are a God who works behind
the scenes, God of Israel, Savior God.
Isaiah 45:15 MSG

Direct me, Lord, to the path that fits in with Your plan—
for the good of myself and all Your children. In Jesus' name, amen.

Rash Requests

The scene is o'er, and the great teacher, Time,
Has cooled the passions 'roused o'er cups of wine.
Amid the cares and splendors of the throne,
The king is sad, disconsolate, alone.

In Esther 2:1 we find our king depressed. The party was over and he was feeling the "fool" effects of what had happened. Sober and cool of head, he regretted his rash request of his queen. Perhaps now he understood why she was reluctant to obey his command to appear before him in a room full of drunken men.

Away from his fellow feasters, Ahasuerus missed his charming wife, whose beauty was beyond compare, and regretted the decree against her. Perhaps he wondered if it could be reversed.

Thinking a reinstated Vashti would quickly separate their bodies from their heads, the king's advisers suggested his loneliness be lessened by finding a new queen. Hearing their suggestions, the king once again was swayed.

Yet we might pause here to compare the rashness of this king to that of another. So we leave the Old Testament for a moment to step into the New. . . .

There once was a king named Herod who was married to Herodias, a woman who was once his brother Philip's wife. John the Baptist had been telling the king, "It is against God's law for you to marry your brother's wife" (Mark 6:18 NLT). Because of his remarks, Herodias wanted to kill John. But she couldn't do so without the king's approval. So she bided her time and was eventually rewarded.

On King Herod's birthday, he had a party for nobles, military leaders, and the upper crust of Galilee. During the celebrations,

Herodias's daughter performed a dance that pleased the guests and king. Afterward he said to her, "Ask for whatever you'd like and I will give it to you—even up to half my kingdom!"

Prompted by her mother, the girl said, "I'd like the head of John the Baptist!"

"Then the king deeply regretted what he had said; but because of the vows he had made in front of his guests, he couldn't refuse her" (Mark 6:26 NLT). And the deed was done.

Two kings. Two parties. Two rash decisions.

Perhaps you have had times when you've made decisions you've regretted. Granted, those decisions may not have involved royal decrees and beheadings. But later you may have rued the rash action you took and could not take back.

God would have His people think before they act, to consult with Him before rendering a decision. Would that God's daughters be wiser than mortal kings.

We are no longer to be children, tossed here and there by waves and carried about by every wind of doctrine, by the trickery of people, by craftiness in deceitful scheming.
EPHESIANS 4:14 NASB

I pray, Lord, that You would help me grow up in my faith and become a wiser woman, not a ruer of rash requests. Amen.

The Matchmaker

The king's decree to every province ran,
And flowers were culled to bloom in gay Shushan.
The princess' garden, and the poor man's field,
Alike are called their choicest rose to yield.

Working behind the scenes, God had set the stage to replace Queen Vashti with a woman who would be much more likely to help save His people. And the king's advisers have laid out their plan to help bring that about.

The kingdom of Ahasuerus would be scoured; beautiful young virgin girls would be sought. The king would appoint officers in all his provinces to bring these young virgins to the harem in the fortress of Susa. These lucky ladies would be under the charge of Hegai, the king's eunuch who oversaw the women. Hegai would take them through a beautification process. And the girl who pleased the king the most would become his new queen in place of Vashti. To this plan the king heartily agreed.

This process sounds like today's series *The Bachelor*, where a single man is presented with and romances a select group of women. From among these women, he will then choose a wife. Like the women of the harem, they're secluded from the rest of the world during the selection process—no cell phones, news, magazines, shopping, social media, or TV. They're to get in the best shape they can physically and, of course, be beautiful. They can't skip any dates or requests. And the station that broadcasts the series is their boss for an entire twelve months.

It appears not much has changed since Esther's day. Some of the harem girls might have had the same challenges faced by contestants on *The Bachelor*.

Yet this way of choosing a mate is not what God had in mind. First, God would have you choose someone who loves Him as much as you do, even if that means going outside of your neighborhood (Genesis 24:1–4). God would have you rely on Him for guidance in finding your mate, expecting "He will send His Angel before you" (Genesis 24:7 AMPC) and confirm the one who He thinks is your perfect match (Genesis 24:12–16). And once you've found that one who lights up your life, He would have you worship Him, blessing and thanking Him for placing His hand on your life (Genesis 24:26–27). Lastly, God would have you not delay in linking your life with his in marriage (Genesis 24:56).

While keeping all that in mind, remember to look for godly character in a man above all other things (Proverbs 31:30). Don't just fall in love with his looks but look deep within his heart (1 Samuel 16:7), knowing that, just as beauty is in a woman, handsomeness in a man is only skin deep.

> *"People judge by outward appearance,*
> *but the LORD looks at the heart."*
> 1 SAMUEL 16:7 NLT

Lord, help me look more at the hearts of
people than at their appearance. Amen.

Hidden in Exile

In Shushan dwelt an honored exiled Jew,
Named Mordecai, within whose garden grew
An only flower; that flower was in full bloom,
And shedding 'round his house its rich perfume.

I n Esther 2:5–6 we get closer to our heroine. For here is where we meet Esther's surrogate father, Mordecai. He is introduced as a Jew named Mordecai, who was "from the tribe of Benjamin and was a descendant of Kish and Shimei" (Esther 2:5 NLT). We're told that "his ancestors had been taken from Jerusalem with the exiles and carried off with King Jehoiachin of Judah by King Nebuchadnezzar of Babylon into exile" (Esther 2:6 MSG).

Mordecai's great-grandfather Kish had been living in Jerusalem under King Jehoiachin of Judah. And that same Kish had been taken captive by Nebuchadnezzar in 597 BC. Then, in 539 BC, when the Persians conquered Babylon, many Jews migrated to the cities in Persia. The following year, 538 BC, Cyrus the Great, king of the Achaemenid Empire, allowed the Jews to return to Jerusalem and rebuild their temple and town. But Mordecai chose to remain in Susa, at this exact time in our story when Ahasuerus is in search of a wife.

In Esther 2:7 we are introduced to Hadassah, aka Esther, the cousin Mordecai raised as his own daughter since her parents had died. And we learn of Esther's two names—Hadassah, Hebrew for "myrtle," and Esther, Persian for "star"—and her description: "The young woman had a beautiful figure and was lovely to look at" (ESV).

This young flower Mordecai had raised, hidden behind his garden wall, had reached full bloom when, as our poet tells us, "the man who gathered fairest flowers passed by / And plucked the only rose of Mordecai."

What timing! How wonderfully God had set the stage for Esther, the beautiful young woman, ripe and ready when the king's men are looking for virgins for their sovereign.

Once again we're reminded of God's machinations behind the curtains of this stage we call the world. For Kish was not killed during any battles or while in exile. He managed to keep his family alive as well, allowing his son Shimei to raise a family, and his son Jair to raise a family, including his son Mordecai—and to raise him in the Hebrew faith. Those efforts, in turn, molded Mordecai into a good man who took over the responsibility of raising his beautiful young cousin under the umbrella of his faith.

Having Esther plucked out of his grasp must have been a cruel blow to Mordecai. But he maintained his faith in God, knowing God's plan was the best plan for him and Esther and, eventually, for *all* of God's children.

> *The Lord's plans stand firm forever;*
> *his intentions can never be shaken.*
> PSALM 33:11 NLT

I rest and relax in the knowledge that You, Lord, have a plan.
Show me the role You would have me play in it. Amen.

The View from Within

The Jewish orphan maiden, reared with care,
With form divine, and face beyond compare,
Came pensive, yielding to the stern decree,
Arrayed in robes of true simplicity.

Living in a foreign country amid people who did not worship their God, the exiled Jews must have felt weak and subservient to their adopted country and its culture. A Jewish woman must have felt even more so, for she did not have the same rights as a man. Add the fact that Esther was an orphaned Jewish female living in exile, and she may have begun to see herself as the weakest of the weak—perhaps even as a victim! And now she was herded up with so many other young girls, taken to live at the palace, and put into the custody of the king's eunuch Hegai. Esther didn't seem to have the upper hand in any aspect of her life.

It's easy to view your life circumstances of birth, social class, sex, situation, and so on as so far beneath others that you can barely lift up your head. Yet that's not what Esther did. She did not let her circumstances determine who she was. Her character and beauty—inner and outer—always came shining through! She retained her dignity, modesty, wisdom, and sense of worth under all circumstances.

Any female might wonder where Esther got her poise, her bravado, her take-it-as-it-comes approach to life. Perhaps much of it came from her upbringing. Although we know little of Esther's parents, we do learn much about Mordecai. He bowed to no one other than his God. He was passionate enough to mourn for his people when he discovered the murderous decree that eventually came against them. And he was courageous enough to stand his ground on several occasions. Such a man didn't have to live in Jerusalem to stay true to his Lord. No matter where he went, he knew his God was with him and would never leave him.

Mordecai's strength, trust, faith, and hope in his God were a daily example to Esther. Perhaps his faithful prayers to God, study of the scriptures, and moments of worship also taught his surrogate daughter where her true power lay—in her almighty God.

These are things all women should embrace in their lives, then pass on to those who come after them. Hold firm to this truth that no matter where we are, no matter what happens in our lives, there is One greater we can count on, One who will shine His light upon our path, One who goes before us and meets us and walks with us where we are. He is the One who teaches us not how to be victims but how to become victors.

> " 'But I,' declares the LORD, 'will be a wall of fire to her
> on all sides, and I will be the glory in her midst.' "
> ZECHARIAH 2:5 NASB

With You within and without, dear Lord, I will be victorious.

The Star Appears!

The inward powers like polished sapphires shine,
And give the tints of heaven to beauty's shrine.
All, all were held in admiration's spell,
Who saw the brilliant star of Israel.

Esther's beauty—within and without—shone the brightest among all those who had been chosen for the king's harem. So bedazzling was her luster that she soon gained special favor from Hegai, the eunuch in charge of the king's women. He promptly started her beauty treatments, provided special food, gave her seven palace maids, and put her in the best rooms.

All this information is strangely offset by the next verse: "Esther had not told anyone of her nationality and family background, because Mordecai had directed her not to do so" (Esther 2:10 NLT).

Here was a jewel of heaven, perhaps the only one in the harem or even the entire fortress, who worshipped the one true God and was well acquainted with His strength, power, and love. She had not become a worshipper of the idols or false gods revered by the Persians. Thus, it's no wonder Mordecai found himself pacing outside every day "beside the court of the harem to find out how Esther was and get news of what she was doing" (Esther 2:11 MSG).

Any parent can understand how Mordecai must have felt. His young daughter, the one for whom he had provided both physical and spiritual shelter, was alone among pagans! Would she be strong enough to keep silent about her family background and nationality and still stay close to her God?

There comes a time in every woman's life when she has to stand alone in the world, away from hearth and home, and make her own way. It's then that her parents hope she will thrive enough not only to feed, clothe, and house herself but to grow even deeper in her faith.

In some nations, Christianity is on the rise. In others, on the decline. Yet we can have faith that God will continue to work out His plan in this world. He will work behind the scenes to raise up women who will be as strong and brave as Esther, ones who appear to be alone, without friends, family, or finances, yet who know the one true God and how He works His will in the lives of women across the globe. We can have faith that as long as we stand with God, we will never be standing alone. And that faith will enable us to be still and know that God's Spirit and power are hovering above the chaos and ushering in the sun-, moon-, and starlight.

The earth was without form and void, and darkness was over the face of the deep. And the Spirit of God was hovering over the face of the waters. And God said, "Let there be light," and there was light.
GENESIS 1:2–3 ESV

In You, Lord Jesus, I am still and find my light. Amen.

Under Wraps

Supreme o'er Gentile virgins Esther shone,
Her people and her country all unknown;
For Mordecai had said: "Thou shalt not tell
Thy kindred 's of the house of Israel."

Mordecai had advised Esther to hide her nationality, her faith, her people (2:10, 20). In effect, a very important part of this child/woman's makeup was still under wraps, hidden from the eyes of all mortals, except Mordecai, and would only be revealed in God's own time.

In this way, Esther is like other hidden heroes, such as Gideon, Joseph, and David.

Gideon was literally hiding from the Midianites, the people who kept invading Israel and taking the best of their beasts and crops. After Gideon's people called out to God, the angel of the Lord paid a call on him while he was threshing wheat in a winepress, out of the sight of his enemies. The angel called him a mighty hero (Judges 6:12)! Then the Lord told him, "Go with the strength you have, and rescue Israel from the Midianites. I am sending you!" (Judges 6:14 NLT).

When Gideon told the Lord he was a member of the weakest clan and the least of his family, God told him to go anyway, for "I will be with you" (Judges 6:16 NLT). Gideon went. God was with him. And the Israelites were rescued.

At the hands of his angry and jealous brothers, Joseph the dreamer was thrown into a cistern in Israel and sold to a caravan of Midianite traders. From there he was taken to Egypt, enslaved, falsely accused of rape, and put in a dungeon. Yet through it all, he stayed close to God. So God stayed close to him, making whatever he did prosper (Genesis 39:3). God then raised him up to be Pharoah's right-hand man, a position enabling Joseph to later save his entire family!

David too was hidden. Once God rejected Saul as king, He sent the prophet Samuel to Jesse and his sons. Warned by God not to judge the future-but-now-hidden king by his appearance or height, Samuel anointed the youngest and least of Jesse's sons: the boy-shepherd named David. After David's anointing, the Spirit of the Lord came upon him. And when his time came, David not only defeated a giant Philistine but outran and outruled King Saul.

Esther too, a daughter of the Lord, stayed under wraps until the timing was exactly right, all so she could successfully save her people.

Just as God used these people for His purposes, to bring forth his plan, God can use you. All you have to do is wait for your day to come. And when it does, He will reveal you at just the right time.

Hegai. . .was overseer of the women. Esther was among them.
ESTHER 2:8 MSG

Lord, here I am, hidden among Your people. Be close to me as I await Your purpose and plan for my life. In Jesus' name, amen.

Blessed in Obedience

Pensive and sad the pious Jew resorts,
And daily walks before the royal courts;
Anxious to know if heaven will kindly aid
In this new scene the much loved orphan maid.

Esther was an obedient daughter to her surrogate father, Mordecai. Esther 2:10 says that she kept her nationality and family background a secret because Mordecai had directed her not to reveal them. A further explanation as to why Esther kept these things hidden is given in Esther 2:20 (NLT): "She was still following Mordecai's directions, just as she did when she lived in his home."

Esther also "never went to the king. . .unless he desired her and summoned her by name" (Esther 2:14 HCSB). Then we are told, "When her turn came to go to the king, she did not ask for anything except what Hegai, the king's trusted official in charge of the harem, suggested" (Esther 2:15 HCSB).

And what was the result of the obedience Esther showed to her surrogate father Mordecai, King Ahasuerus, and Hegai? Not only did she win "approval in the sight of everyone who saw her" (2:15 HCSB), but "she won more favor and approval from [the king] than did any of the other young women" (2:17 HCSB)!

Esther truly sounds like a willingly humble and obedient person. She knew that those who loved her would give her guidelines and advice not to curtail her freedom or to lord power over her, but rather to ensure she would get the best there was to offer! She knew that when she humbly obeyed those who were wiser, those who had the best in mind for her, good things would come to her.

Mordecai continued to watch over her as best he could, every day taking "a walk near the courtyard of the harem to find out about Esther and what was happening to her" (Esther 2:11 NLT). And on the inside of the palace, Hegai, the king's eunuch in charge of the harem in Susa, "treated her kindly" (Esther 2:9 NLT), ordering her special food and beauty treatments and giving her the best rooms and maids. All her humility and obedience brought her nothing but good!

Just as Mordecai and Hegai watched over Esther, God watches over His obedient children. Although you may not see Him outside or inside your own "palace," you can be sure He's wherever you are and interested in how you're faring.

Simply and humbly obey your Lord, and good will follow. For all God expects from you is your obedience.

Live in his presence in holy reverence, follow the road he sets out for you, love him, serve GOD, your God, with everything you have in you, obey the commandments and regulations of GOD that I'm commanding you today—live a good life.
DEUTERONOMY 10:12–13 MSG

Help me, Lord, to become obedient to You, knowing You always have the best in mind for me. Amen.

Esther Rises

And thus Queen Esther came in royal state,
To save the exiled Jews from dismal fate.
The ways of Providence are dark and high,
And who can scan the God of sovereignty?

We now come to the juncture where God had placed Esther into the position of power needed to save the lives of His people. For the king had fallen head over heels, loving Esther "more than any of the other young women. He was so delighted with her that he set the royal crown on her head and declared her queen instead of Vashti" (Esther 2:17 NLT).

Here we must once again remember and take note that God's divine hand was all the time overruling the purposes and passions of all the players in Esther's story. So far in her tale, God has orchestrated the king's banquet request and Vashti's refusal, both of which have paved the way for a woman believed to be Persian, but who is actually Jewish, to come to power as Ahasuerus's new queen.

Yet the Highest Power's name is neither written nor spoken within Esther's book. He still works behind the scenes as her history unfolds moment by moment, word by word. About this J. B. Steele writes in *Sacred Poetical Paraphrases, and Miscellaneous Poems,*

> *The reading of this wonderful story is well*
> *calculated to lead the mind to the contemplation*
> *of the character of our heavenly Father, who*
> *controls all hearts, and orders all events in such*
> *a manner as to promote His own glory, and*
> *secure the salvation of the Church. The wheels of*

Providence very often appear to us
high and dreadful, but by careful study,
and patient observation, we can discover
a wheel within a wheel, manifesting the
special care of God, not only over us as a whole,
but over the most humble individual Christian.

We also must consider what may have been going through the minds of Mordecai and Esther. As exiles in a pagan nation, they must have wondered what plan God was working to bring this young Israelite to a place of such power. What could these happenings portend? What momentous occasion were these events leading up to? And what might happen if Esther were found to be a Jewess before she herself revealed her secret?

All these what-ifs can bring us to a place of fear rather than a place of wonder. At this point all we can really do is trust that God will make all known in time. And as long as we are open to His voice and obedient to it, all will be more than well. For He has told us:

"No weapon that is fashioned against you shall succeed."
ISAIAH 54:17 ESV

Help me, Lord, not to worry myself with what-ifs
but to be confident in what is. For You are
in control of all. In Jesus' name, amen.

A Contagion of Kindness

The king was generous on that joyful day.
Far as extends his wide extended sway
His royal gifts are sent. A firm release
The provinces receive, and heavy burdens cease.

E sther's humility won the hearts of many in her life, beginning with that of Mordecai. Since the day he took in his orphaned cousin, his love was won over by her vulnerability.

Esther, reared in the knowledge and wonder of the One who ruled over all men and women, soon became unquestionably obedient to her spiritual Lord and to her cousin Mordecai who had now taken the role of father in her life. He taught her about their God in word and led by example. And that was how she learned kindness—not just to those above her but particularly to those below her.

It was this kindness of Esther's, along with her humility and obedience, that found her favor with all, including her newest and latest convert, the king himself. Yes, Ahasuerus, who hitherto has been described as full of pride, loving to display his wealth, at times a heavy drinker and a fool, a man with a temper, a bit spoiled, fickle, unable to control himself, rash in judgments, receptive to bad advice, easily persuaded, and rueful when sober. None of these are characteristics to brag about. That's why it's so striking to read that "the king loved Esther more than all the women, and she found favor and kindness with him more than all the virgins" (Esther 2:17 NASB). It appears Esther brought out the best in those with whom she came into contact! Her own kindness, which she had learned from Mordecai, was now "caught" by this king who, as far as personality and behaviors go, had nothing much to recommend him!

And soon his kindness exploded out into the kingdom! To celebrate his beautiful new young bride and queen, Ahasuerus "gave a great feast for all his officials and servants; it was Esther's feast. He also granted a remission of taxes to the provinces and gave gifts with royal generosity" (Esther 2:18 ESV).

Ruth, the only other Bible book named after a woman, is another example of how kindness begets kindness. For it was the widowed Ruth who showed compassion to her widowed mother-in-law, Naomi, sticking with her when she made that long trek back to Israel, then providing for Naomi by gleaning in a relative's field. And it was that same kindness of Ruth's that attracted the field's owner, Boaz, who was kind to Ruth in return.

Today, may you start your own contagion of kindness—not for the reward but for the pleasure it affords.

"Those who show loving-kindness are happy,
because they will have loving-kindness shown to them."
MATTHEW 5:7 NLV

Lord, help me catch Your kindness more and more
so that I can spread it to others—and start
my own contagion of kindness. Amen.

A Plot Uncovered

The king's unconscious of the deadly hate
Of faithless chamberlains, who watching wait
The favored time, like hungry wolves, to spring
And glut their vengeance on th' unguarded king.

*E*sther had been crowned queen. In Esther 2:20 the author of her story reminds us of how she continued to be obedient to Mordecai by keeping secret their nationality and faith, staying just as faithful to him as she had been in childhood.

The next verse then relates a plot that Mordecai overheard. Apparently, he was sitting at the King's Gate as two of the king's servants, eunuchs Bigthan and Teresh, guarded the doorway. They expressed anger and spoke of plans to kill King Ahasuerus.

What these two servants were up in arms about is unknown. Some scholars speculate these eunuchs may have been loyal to Vashti, the former queen. Perhaps to avenge her honor or to retaliate against her ill treatment by the king, they plotted to kill him. Regardless of their true motives, their plan became known to Mordecai. And once he received the knowledge, he passed it on to his adopted daughter, Queen Esther. She, in turn, told the king what Mordecai had learned.

When the plot was investigated and verified, the men were hanged on the gallows. The entire affair was then "written down in the Book of the Chronicles in front of the king" (Esther 2:23 NLV).

This entire subplot is related in only three verses. And although it is interesting, it is quickly passed over. Yet it contains elements that will be built upon, as almost all events that make up our lives normally do.

How often do you find that seemingly trivial events, ones that are soon forgotten, later end up being integral to a success, failure, or change of circumstances in your own life? Granted, two men plotting to kill a king may not sound insignificant to you. Yet if you lived in a kingdom, perhaps even within a palace in the days of Esther, plots against the king may have seemed commonplace.

The point is that we never know what evil intentions or disappointments may work together to bring about something good in the long run. We never know when or how our measures, our intent to do the right thing, will be rewarded. We never know what import our routine actions—like recording an event in a book, journal, or ledger—will have in the end. We never know what steps God will take or what means He will use to bring about His plans and purposes. All we can do is keep walking the right way, knowing God will work all things out.

"You intended to harm me, but God intended it all for good."
Genesis 50:20 NLT

Help me, Lord, to rest in the fact that You are
in control over all the events in my life and
will make all things work for my good. Amen.

Seven Devils in One

At his right hand the king has placed the seat
Of Hammedatha's son, the proud, the great.
O'er all the princes, all the men of might,
Sits high enthroned Haman the Amalekite.

I n Esther 3 we meet one of the most infamous characters in history—Haman. Of him, Alexander Whyte writes,

> *Haman, the son of Hammedatha the Agagite, was*
> *seven devils rolled into one. He was a very devil of*
> *pride, and of jealousy, and of revenge, and of an*
> *insatiable thirst for Hebrew blood. How almighty*
> *God should have let so many devils loose in one*
> *devil-possessed man is another mystery of His*
> *power, and wisdom, and judgment, and love. But*
> *there it is, as plain as inspired words can write it.*

So who exactly is this Haman, the son of Hammedatha, and what was an Agagite?

All we know for certain is that his father's name was Hammedatha. As far as Haman being an Agagite, there are three positions. The first is that he was descended from Agag, king of the Amalekites (the family of Esau's grandson Amalek), adversaries of the Jews whom God cursed (Genesis 36:12; Exodus 17:14; 1 Samuel 15:8–18).

The second is that "Agagite" is more of an allegorical nickname than a name implying actual and natural descent. In other words, Haman's attitude and actions were like those of Agag and his ilk. The third is that it's anybody's guess. Perhaps "Agagite" is a family name or the name of his hometown. Regardless of where Haman's nomenclature came from or how it pertained to him or his heritage, his actions and words tell us all we need to know. He. Was. Evil.

Haman first comes to our attention as the person whom King Ahasuerus raised to a high position, far above all his contemporaries. And because of Haman's position and the customs of that day, the king commanded that all his servants bow down to Haman. But one man would neither bow down to him nor treat him with great honor. That one man was Mordecai.

Three vastly different men appear in this account. The first is a king with low morals and high pride, lacking in wisdom but abounding in misdemeanors. The second is Mordecai, a man with a great heart, great wisdom, and great understanding, who will not bow to anyone or anything, unless that one is God. The third is Haman, a greedy man with a huge ego, a lust for revenge, and the desire to be treated like a god.

And somehow God will work behind the scenes, using extraordinary events and an unlikely cast of characters to not only protect His people but extinguish their enemy.

> *Do not get upset because of evildoers, do not be*
> *envious of wrongdoers. For they will wither quickly*
> *like the grass, and decay like the green plants.*
> PSALM 37:1–2 NASB

Help me, Lord, not to worry about those who do evil but to remember You will make sure they come to nothing in the end.

Steadfast Mordecai

The sacred honors which alone are given
To the high Power who rules in earth and heaven,
To man the Benjamite will not bestow,
And Mordecai to Haman will not bow.

$a$lthough to bow the knee and pay homage to great people was a common custom in Persia, the king need not have commanded such behavior toward Haman. Yet he did so anyway, giving the impression that Haman had endeared himself to Ahasuerus. Thus, it seemed even more of an affront to the wicked and prideful Haman that Mordecai did not make any move to show him respect.

Mordecai of the Benjamite tribe could not in good conscience slight his own God by bowing to any man, much less one of Haman's evil ilk (Esther 3:2). Paying homage to such a person would have been like slapping God across the face! It was not to be done!

This gives us more insight into the kind of man Mordecai was. Even though he was an alien in the land, far from his family home of Israel, he remained steadfast to his God, unwilling to bend the knee to a mere mortal.

Mordecai's refusal to pay homage to Haman is not unlike the actions of three other Jewish exiles—Shadrach, Meshach, and Abednego. Babylon's King Nebuchadnezzar had set up a golden statue. When the musical cue was given, all people were to fall down to this idol and worship it immediately. If they did not, they would be thrown into a fiery furnace (Daniel 3:4–6).

All people obeyed this proclamation except Shadrach, Meshach, and Abednego. When the enraged king questioned the trio about their disobedience, threatening them with a fiery demise, their only response was: "If we are thrown into the blazing furnace, the God whom we serve is able to save us. He will rescue us from your power. . . . But even if he doesn't, we want to make it clear to you, Your Majesty, that we will never serve your gods or worship the gold statue you have set up" (Daniel 3:17–18 NLT).

In response, the king had the three friends thrown into the fiery furnace. But when he looked into the flames, he saw not three but four men walking around, the fourth being like a son of God. And when the door was opened, the three men came out, unscathed and not even smelling of smoke.

Joshua had told the Israelites not to turn from the word of God, neither calling on the gods of other nations nor worshipping or bowing down to them (Joshua 23:6–8). May we, along with Mordecai, Shadrach, Meshach, and Abednego, find the strength and determination to worship only the one true God.

> *"Remain faithful to the LORD your God,*
> *as you have done to this day."*
> JOSHUA 23:8 HCSB

> *To You alone, my God and Savior,*
> *I drop on bended knee.*

Social, State, and Spiritual Laws

"I am a Jew; from God's most holy law
My principles of faith and life I draw;
All civil honors to the prince I bring,
But reverence yield to Heaven's eternal King."

For Mordecai not to pay homage to Haman was one thing. To have his insubordination witnessed by others was another. Some of the king's other servants who were part of the royal staff and were at the King's Gate asked Mordecai day after day, "Why are you disobeying the king's command?" (Esther 3:3 HCSB).

While we're not sure exactly how Mordecai responded to this question, we do know that he, at the very least, told them he was a Jew. For it was with that information these same servants of the king went to Haman, wanting to see "if Mordecai's actions would be tolerated, since he had told them he was a Jew" (Esther 3:4 HCSB).

Here we have three laws in conflict: social, state, and spiritual. The social laws or mores of Persia in that day were that those in power were to be held in high regard by either bending the knee or bowing to them. The state laws (in this case the king's commands) were to be obeyed no matter what. And in this instance, King Ahasuerus had commanded *all* the king's servants to bow down to and pay homage to Haman (Esther 3:2). But spiritual laws set by God forbid such behavior. For the God of Israel was known to be a jealous God (Exodus 20:5; Joshua 23:6–8). Thus, Mordecai resisted any and all attempts to betray his one and only Lord and Master.

Such conflicts between social, state, and spiritual laws were experienced by Peter and the other apostles who, after healing many in Jerusalem, were arrested by the high priest. But an angel of the Lord freed them from jail in the middle of the night, instructing them to go to the temple and teach the Good News. The next day, they were brought before the high priest and his supporters and asked, "Didn't we tell you not to teach in Jesus' name?" Peter and his fellow apostles replied, "We must obey God rather than men" (Acts 5:29 HCSB).

Perhaps you too have found your spirit in conflict with today's customs or state laws. Perhaps you've been pressured by peers to do something you know is against God's ways.

Yet God would have you remain obedient to Him above all others. He would have you come to Him, look into His Word, and pray not only for His guidance, will, and wisdom but also for the strength to be like Mordecai, faithful to God alone and taking a fixed, unshaken stand.

> *My foot has held fast to His steps;*
> *His ways have I kept and not turned aside.*
> JOB 23:11 AMPC

Lord, help me to remain true to You above anyone or anything else. You alone are the One I follow. Amen.

Anger Overboard

When the vain glorious courtier heard and knew,
That he who bowed not was a pious Jew,
His soul was full of wrath; and knowing well
That the same feeling ruled in Israel,
He scorned the death alone of Mordecai,
But doomed the nation by the sword to die.

Haman wasn't just a bit peeved that Mordecai wouldn't bow to him. He wasn't just insulted. He was totally and completely enraged, which led to his outrage.

And, yes, there is a difference. To be *enraged* is to be filled with rage, to be provoked to fury or madness. An *outrage* is an unreasonably violent or brutal attack, an atrocity. Haman's anger made him go overboard, wanting not just to crush a Jew named Mordecai. No, that would never be enough to appease Haman's anger. He would have to destroy *all* Jews.

When any person's expectations are dashed, all hell can literally break out. Matthew Henry writes, "By nature all are idolaters; self is our favourite idol, we are pleased to be treated as if every thing were at our disposal. Though religion by no means destroys good manners, but teaches us to render honour to whom honour is due." He goes on to point out that "the true believer cannot obey edicts, or conform to fashions, which break the law of God. He must obey God rather than man, and leave the consequences to him."*

For some of us, obeying God and then leaving the results in His hands can be difficult. For we build up ideas in our minds of how things should be, allowing no room for God to shape us within or work His own plan without. When our expectations then fall short, we wonder why. We then begin to envy those who have what we don't. We wonder where God is and why our hope has been deferred, our prayers unanswered. We begin to feel sorry for ourselves and perhaps lash out in anger at those closest to us for our unmet expectations.

Thank the Lord we can, in such situations, turn to the Word for guidance. For there we're told to trust in God, to delight ourselves in Him, knowing then He will give us the desires of our heart. We're to commit our ways to the Lord, lean on Him, trust Him. And most of all, we're to "cease from anger and forsake wrath; fret not. . .it tends only to evildoing" (Psalm 37:8 AMPC).

Unlike Haman, who was a god in his own eyes, we're to look away from all that might distract us—our disappointments, frustrations, worries, and anger—and keep "our eyes on Jesus. . .who for the joy that lay before Him endured a cross and despised the shame and has sat down at the right hand of God's throne" (Hebrews 12:2 HCSB).

> *Be still in the presence of the LORD,*
> *and wait patiently for him to act.*
> PSALM 37:7 NLT

Lord, I entrust all I am and all I long for to You.

*Matthew Henry, Matthew Henry's Concise Commentary on the Bible, biblehub.com/commentaries/esther/3-3.htm

Gambling with Fate

Thus Haman's soul with vengeful passion burns,
And now to work his ends his fiery spirit turns.
The heathen oracle shall set the time
To execute the dark, the vast design.

The enraged Haman had designed his plan to obliterate not only Mordecai, the Jew who would not bow to him, but all Jews throughout Ahasuerus's kingdom. Now all that was left to determine was the timing of the mass eradication of God's people. So what did this pagan Persian official do? "Haman caused Pur, that is, lots, to be cast before him day after day [to find a lucky day for his venture], month after month, until the twelfth, the month of Adar" (Esther 3:7 AMPC).

The lots were cast for Haman by the king's wise men or astrologers. And there was something very interesting about the date they arrived at as being "lucky" for Haman. The month in which the plot to annihilate the Jews was to be implemented was also the month marking their wondrous deliverance from Egypt!

But that's not all! As it turns out, the date chosen was an entire *year* away—giving Mordecai and Esther ample time to prevent the mass execution of their people. Yes, the date chosen, the date Haman had gambled on, was lucky indeed.

Who knows who Haman prayed to when the lots were being cast. Perhaps to Lady Luck. But we who are God's people know there is no such thing as luck. For although lots may be cast and dice thrown, or motions made and votes cast, we know that in all such things "God has the final say" (Proverbs 16:33 MSG)—and we must abide by whatever He determines.

Deducing lucky and unlucky days, attempting to tell fortunes, and other such practices have existed for millennia. But we are to turn our eyes and hopes away from such traditions. God clearly spells it out within His word: "Do not let your people practice fortune-telling, or use sorcery, or interpret omens, or engage in witchcraft, or cast spells, or function as mediums or psychics, or call forth the spirits of the dead" (Deuteronomy 18:10–11 NLT). Why does God forbid such methods? Because He wants us to look to Him—as well as His Son—for all those things! That's why Jesus left us with the Holy Spirit, our Comforter, Counselor, Helper, Intercessor, Advocate, Strength, and Standby. We are to take Him, the Spirit of Truth—whom the world doesn't see, know, or recognize—into our hearts where He will dwell with us continually (John 14:16–17).

Turn away from lucky days, fortune-telling, astrology, and other such superstitions. Instead, lean into the Spirit of truth, knowing all outcomes are determined by the Lord.

The lot is cast into the lap,
but its every decision is from the LORD.
PROVERBS 16:33 NASB

I entrust my lot to You, Lord,
for You hold all the cards.

Fitting Truths

The time arranged, the favorite courtier stands
Before the throne, to obtain the king's commands,
The royal order, and the sealed decree,
To bring about the awful massacre.

Haman has determined the plan and the date. The next step is to persuade the king to go along with his grand scheme. Thus, Haman approaches his sovereign's throne, where he soon finds a way to mingle the truth with a lie or two.

Haman says to Ahasuerus, "There is an odd set of people scattered through the provinces of your kingdom who don't fit in. Their customs and ways are different from those of everybody else. Worse, they disregard the king's laws. They're an affront; the king shouldn't put up with them" (Esther 3:8 MSG).

The first two sentences of Haman's argument are true. The Jews, who must have appeared odd to their Persian counterparts, were scattered throughout Ahasuerus's kingdom. Chances are their ways and manners were different from all others. That's where the truth ends—and where Haman's lies begin. For the Jews did not disregard the king's laws.

Granted, one Jew named Mordecai did refuse to bow to Haman. But Mordecai is one among many! Thus, Haman is using a lie to feed his sovereign's ego—to get Ahasuerus up in arms about an untrue scenario. In effect, Haman was initializing, presenting, and spreading fake news! All to get his own way, to wreak vengeance against the one man who had injured his pride.

We're faced with two considerations here. The first is that we, like the Jews, are to be a people separate from the world

(Deuteronomy 14:2; 1 Peter 2:9). For the Lord has set apart the godly for Himself (Psalm 4:3). The second is that we are to stand apart from the world, from unbelievers (2 Corinthians 6:17). Are you? Are you different from the world? Do other people see you as out of place, out of step with the rest of society? If so, God is pleased! Not that you're to be odd just to be odd. But you're not to be like the rest of the world, clamoring for first place, full of pride and conceit, stepping on others to get ahead. You're to stand out by being humble, worshipping God rather than the almighty dollar, speaking in truth, and focusing on Jesus.

As a Christ follower, you're not supposed to "fit in" with the rest of the world but to allow God to transform you into His daughter who looks to do His will and walk His way—and speak and spread the truth as you do so. For you worship a God of truth, one who will brook no lies from the mouths of His children.

Don't copy the behavior and customs of this world, but let God transform you into a new person by changing the way you think.
ROMANS 12:2 NLT

God of truth and love, transform me into a woman who is honest and humble, a woman who is after Your own heart.

The Danger of a Single Story

"O king, within thy provinces are found
A certain race, scattered, dispersed around;
With laws that differ from the Persian laws,
And rites injurious to the public cause.
A race that do not honor, or fulfill
The royal statutes, or the sovereign will."

Haman stands before Ahasuerus and begins his narrative: "There is an odd set of people scattered through the provinces of your kingdom who don't fit in. Their customs and ways are different from those of everybody else. Worse, they disregard the king's laws. They're an affront; the king shouldn't put up with them. If it please the king, let orders be given that they be destroyed" (Esther 3:8–9 MSG). He starts with two sentences that ring true.

Then Haman adds some lies to his narrative, saying, "They disregard the king's laws." The word *they* is untrue. It was one person, one man, one Jew whose faith would not allow him to bow his head to a man such as Haman. He, Mordecai, is one man. He does not make a "they."

On that mistruth, Haman builds his story—a single story with a single perspective: "These Jews, unlawful oddballs, cannot be tolerated. They are an affront to you and so must be destroyed." Before King Ahasuerus checked out these claims, before he asked for other opinions from his advisers or did his own research, he was signing a decree to massacre an entire race of people!

This is a prime example of what happens when you read only one story or scan its contents too quickly, not looking for other information to either confirm or contradict it. It's as if you listen to or read only one news source and don't look any further for other perspectives. Soon you find yourself buying into a false narrative, making erroneous judgments, spouting opinions that have no basis in fact.

Like Esther, who was not just some queen of Persia, a Jewess who made it big, or a woman out for revenge, you yourself are not a single story. You are not just a woman but a follower of Christ. You are not just a voter but a mother concerned about the environment your children will one day inherit. You are not one way, one shape, one color, one degree, or one marital status. You're a complex individual with her own wants, needs, concerns, stories, DNA, and history.

God would not have you so narrowly defined as just another housewife or laborer or divorcee. You are a multifaceted human being with values and dreams that are unique to you alone. And most likely you are someone who wouldn't want a single story told about you. So take care when hearing one story. Always look for another side.

> *Spouting off before listening to the*
> *facts is both shameful and foolish.*
> PROVERBS 18:13 NLT

Lord, give me the wisdom to seek the truth in every story.

Planners of Evil

"Our king's and country's welfare now demands
The race should perish from the Persian lands.
That they may be destroyed a writing seal.
Our nation's glory, and our country's weal,
Shall far extended be, and I will bring
Ten thousand talents to enrich the king."

Here we have one man, Haman, whose pride had been offended and his ego enraged when one Jew by the name of Mordecai refused to bow to him. And now, to satisfy his personal grudge, this one man, Haman, was ready to destroy an entire nation, all of God's people living within the borders of the Persian Empire.

In Esther 3:9 we find Haman proposing his plan for this nation's destruction, and the false reason for its obliteration, to King Ahasuerus. To make the annihilation of the Jews more palatable to the king, Haman offered to pay for the privilege of initiating this holocaust. Apparently a very wealthy man, he proposed to pay into the king's coffers 10,000 talents—more than two-thirds of one year's revenue for the king! Haman was hoping to recoup his talents from the spoils of the Jews who would be slaughtered.

Poor misguided Haman. Little did he know who he was up against. The prophet Micah (2:1–3 NLT) warned what would happen to people of Haman's ilk:

> *What sorrow awaits you who lie awake at night,*
> *thinking up evil plans. You rise at dawn and hurry*
> *to carry them out, simply because you have the*
> *power to do so. When you want a piece of land, you*

find a way to seize it. When you want someone's
house, you take it by fraud and violence. You
cheat a man of his property, stealing his family's
inheritance. But this is what the LORD says: "I will
reward your evil with evil; you won't be able to pull
your neck out of the noose. You will no longer walk
around proudly, for it will be a terrible time."

Haman's scheming against a man of faith such as Mordecai is similar in some aspects to Judas's plotting against Jesus. Both were betrayers to people of God, both dealt with blood money, and both had a last supper before they met their respective demises. But as God reveals through Micah, He promises to reward such people's evil with evil. Neither betrayer would be able to pull his neck out of the noose he had prepared for himself (Esther 7:1–10; Matthew 26:20–27:5).

Leave all vengeance in God's hands. Simply work to carry out the tasks He would have you do each day, and leave the demise of vicious schemers, as well as their evil plans, to God.

> Don't insist on getting even; that's not for you to do.
> "I'll do the judging," says God. "I'll take care of it."
> ROMANS 12:19 MSG

---

*Lord, thank You for protecting Your faithful followers
from evil schemers and doers. Help me leave it to
You to serve up their just desserts. Amen.*

A Box Ticker

The prayer is granted, and the ring is given.
How strange are thy decrees, O God of Heaven!
The greatest monarch on earth's proudest throne
Has given thy flock to Hammedatha's son,
The Agagite, and he will flash his sword
In triumph in the people of the Lord!

Haman's plotting looked like it was going to pay off! Ahasuerus had granted him permission to kill all the Jews in the kingdom, "confirming his decision by removing his signet ring from his finger and giving it to Haman son of Hammedatha the Agagite, the enemy of the Jews. The king said, 'The money and the people are both yours to do with as you see fit' " (Esther 3:10–11 NLT).

This is the sort of scene that makes believers' stomachs turn. They're not alone. God's stomach turns even more because He absolutely *detests* devious people (Proverbs 3:32).

Proverbs 6:16–19 gives us a list of "six things the Lord hates. . .seven are an abomination to Him" (verse 16 AMPC). And Haman was on his way to ticking every single box.

One: "A proud look [the spirit that makes one overestimate himself and underestimate others]" (verse 17 AMPC). Haman's spirit of pride definitely overestimated himself and underestimated not just Mordecai and God's people, but God Himself!

Two: "A lying tongue" (verse 17 AMPC). Haman had already lied to the king by misrepresenting the lawfulness of God's people.

Three: "Hands that shed innocent blood" (verse 17 AMPC). If Haman's edict was carried out, he would effectively be murdering the entire Jewish nation, who were not guilty of lawlessness.

Four: "A heart that manufactures wicked thoughts and plans" (verse 18 AMPC). This edict Haman urged and bribed King Ahasuerus to sign was just the first scheme he plotted.

Five: "Feet that are swift in running to evil" (verse 18 AMPC). We're told of Haman learning about Mordecai's refusal to bow in Esther 3:5. In the very next verse, Haman, learning of Mordecai's ethnicity, "decided not to do away with Mordecai alone. He planned to destroy all of Mordecai's people, the Jews, throughout Ahasuerus's kingdom" (HCSB). What a sprinter!

Six: "A false witness who breathes out lies" (verse 19 AMPC). Again, lying about the Jews, saying they broke the king's laws. And lastly. . .

Seven: "He who sows discord among his brethren" (verse 19 AMPC). Haman's scheme of Persians killing Jews was ultimately reversed to Jews killing Persians. Talk about discord!

The wisdom of Proverbs helps us delineate behavior God hates and behavior He loves. And you can be sure that when you live from the heart, with love at your very core, you will stay on the right side of God's ledger.

> *The devious are an abomination to the LORD;*
> *but He is intimate with the upright.*
> PROVERBS 3:32 NASB

Lord God, make me a woman of wisdom, one who walks in Your will and way. For I long to be intimate with You. Amen.

Stand Still

Stand still and see the works that God will do,
To crush th' oppressor, and exalt the Jew.

Haman's plan for vengeance, the balm to soothe his wounded pride, had been set in motion and appeared to be a scheme that could not be reversed. For he, the king's favorite, the nobleman above all nobles, had gained the king's blessing for his evil plans. And once the king's seal appeared on an edict, it could not be rescinded (Esther 8:8)!

A lot of things in life, evils that have been set in motion, can appear to us humans as juggernauts—huge, powerful, overwhelming forces that can be neither stopped nor reversed. Our prayers for their removal or reversal seem to go unheeded. Feeling helpless and hopeless, we may end up in a pit of despair emotionally, mentally, and spiritually. To find the strength to stand and the hope to endure, we must look to God's Word and remember who He is.

Soon after the formerly enslaved Israelites left Egypt, they found themselves suddenly between Pharaoh and the Red Sea, with seemingly no way out. That's when Moses told them, "Fear not; stand still (firm, confident, undismayed) and see the salvation of the Lord which He will work for you today" (Exodus 14:13 AMPC). Then the Angel of God moved. Taking the form of a cloud that lit up the night, He went behind the Israelites, standing in the breach between His children and the Egyptian chariots.

Moses then raised his hands and God drove the waters back, dividing the sea so the Israelites could pass on dry ground and come out safely on the other side. When the Egyptians entered the sea, hot on the heels of their former slaves, God threw them into confusion, then told Moses to stretch his hands back to close the waters up. He did so, and the mighty force that had dared lift its hand against God's children drowned.

God shows His people time and time again that they should never count Him out. That they should remember, know, depend on the fact that He is always working behind the scenes—and sometimes right in front of them. He can turn what seems to be an irreversible course around so that His people are the victors and their enemies crushed.

God is the only true juggernaut there is. And because He is on our side, we need not be afraid or worried. All we need to do is stand still and watch Him work.

Of course, there will be times when He will call us into action. But the final touches of His saving us will be in His hands, accomplished and worked out as only He can bring to pass.

All we need to do is continue to trust and hope in Him.

> *"Don't be afraid. Just stand still and*
> *watch the LORD rescue you today."*
> EXODUS 14:13 NLT

> *With my hope and trust in You, Lord,*
> *I stand still to watch You move. Amen.*

The Devil in the Details

Not sparing age, or sex, or rank, to slay
The Jewish race, and all their substance hold,
The soldiers' portion, and the spoilers' gold.
The bloody edict spreads abroad, yea flies,
Awaking wrath, and fears, and agonies.

The devilishness of Haman and his plan was found in the details of the king's edict. Between Haman's lust for vengeance and Ahasuerus's negligence or lack of conscience, "bulletins were sent out by couriers to all the king's provinces with orders to massacre, kill, and eliminate all the Jews—youngsters and old men, women and babies—on a single day, the thirteenth day of the twelfth month, the month Adar, and to plunder their goods" (Esther 3:13 MSG).

One might wonder how people can be such monsters at times. It's hard to fathom that one could order such a slaughter of people—and actually force others to carry out those orders! But history teaches us that such people "who plan evil in their hearts" (Psalm 140:2 HCSB) do indeed exist and are walking in our midst today. In his psalm, David describes wicked schemers this way: "They sharpen their tongues like a serpent's; adders' poison is under their lips" (Psalm 140:3 AMPC).

Christians are familiar with such serpents, especially one in particular. He has been around since the beginning. He is the one who was craftier than any other creature the Lord God had made. He is the one who has been lying (and promoting lying) since day one. And the first person he addressed was a woman who swallowed his story hook, line, and sinker.

In Isaiah, God talks about His own people whose sins and lies have separated them from Him. About them, God says, "They conceive mischief and bring forth evil! They hatch adders' eggs and weave the spider's web; he who eats of their eggs dies, and [from an egg] which is crushed a viper breaks out [for their nature is ruinous, deadly, evil]" (Isaiah 59:4–5 AMPC).

John the Baptist and Jesus Himself came across some vipers in the form of Pharisees, Sadducees, and scribes (Matthew 3:7; 23:33). But we can find assurance and comfort in the fact that in the end, "this great dragon—the ancient serpent called the devil, or Satan, the one deceiving the whole world—was thrown down to the earth with all his angels" (Revelation 12:9 NLT).

Yes, Haman's maliciousness, enabled by a negligent king, had set in motion a plan that would be difficult to revoke. But thankfully, we have weapons against such plans. We have the power of our faith and our prayers. Most of all, we have a mighty God on our side (Psalm 118:6–9)—and His plan always prevails.

> *The LORD's arm is not too weak to save you,*
> *nor is his ear too deaf to hear you call.*
> ISAIAH 59:1 NLT

With You on my side, Lord, I fear nothing! Amen.

Special Delivery

To every province of the vast domain
The king's unchangeable commandment came. . . .
The bloody edict spreads abroad, yea flies,
Awaking wrath, and fears, and agonies.

The bloody edict to wipe out all of God's people was in writing and had been sent out. Not just in the Persian province that was home to Mordecai, the original offender of Haman, but all throughout the Persian kingdom.

The edict was written in the name of King Ahasuerus and sealed with his signet ring. The exact details were laid out not just in one language but in *all* the languages of the people. They were "to destroy, to slay, and to do away with all Jews, both young and old, little children and women, in one day, the thirteenth day of the twelfth month, the month of Adar, and to seize their belongings as spoil. A copy of the writing was to be published and given out as a decree in every province to all the peoples to be ready for that day" (Esther 3:13–14 AMPC).

The timing of the mass annihilation of the Jews had been set by lot. The timing of the letter's delivery had been set by Haman. For he'd wanted the seemingly irreversible edict to be sent out before the king changed his mind!

You may be envisioning Haman sneering, snickering, and twirling the ends of his mustache. Or perhaps even rubbing his hands together as if washing them with invisible water, saying to himself, "Yes, yes, yes, it's all going to plan. Not only will I destroy the worm Mordecai, but I will make his entire race disappear!"

What the man failed to recognize or consider was the power of

God, the Lord who so carefully watches over and guards His children. *And* he missed the fact that he had just given God's people the details of his scheme as well as an entire year to find a way to escape the trap Haman had set. Not that they could run, at this point. For if they did, the holocaust would just start earlier, for they would be seen as trying to escape the king's decree.

The writer of Proverbs speaks to such ne'er-do-wells as Haman: "Their feet run toward trouble and they hurry to commit murder. It is foolish to spread a net where any bird can see it, but they set an ambush to kill themselves; they attack their own lives" (Proverbs 1:16–18 HCSB).

Thank God for the ignorance and stupidity of vicious villains who fall into their own pits in their rush to do evil. And thank God for His protection of His people.

> *My soul finds shelter and safety in You, and in the*
> *shadow of Your wings I will take refuge. . . . I will cry*
> *to God Most High, Who accomplishes all things on my*
> *behalf [for He completes my purpose in His plan].*
> PSALM 57:1–2 AMP

> *When I am afraid, Lord, remind me that*
> *I can find refuge and safety in You.*

Persia's Perplexity

In Shushan terror reigns; both foe and friend,
Perplexed, stand wondering where the scene will end
While Haman and the king, to waste the time,
Enjoy the feast and sit o'er cups of wine.

Once the evil proclamation had been received by everyone in the kingdom, confusion reigned. Matthew Poole, in his Bible commentary, writes:

> *The city Shushan was perplexed; not only the Jews,*
> *but a great number of the citizens, either because*
> *they were related to them, or engaged with them*
> *in worldly concerns; or out of humanity and*
> *compassion towards so vast a number of innocent*
> *people, now appointed as sheep for the slaughter;*
> *or out of a fear either of some sedition and*
> *disturbance which might arise by this means;*
> *or of some damage which might accrue to*
> *themselves or friends, who haply under this*
> *pretence might be exposed to rapine or slaughter;*
> *or of a public judgment of God upon them*
> *all for so bloody a decree.**

Some Persians may have wondered what their king was thinking to not just allow and promote but actually authorize a massacre like this on such a large scale! The whole scheme was unsettling to all peoples. Who knew who might be next to suffer at the whims of King Ahasuerus!

Meanwhile, back in the palace, Haman was doing all he could

to keep the king in good spirits, to distract him from any second thoughts or sentiments he might be entertaining on behalf of the Jewish people. Thus, Haman and the king had a fine time sitting down to drink some bottles of wine while confusion reigned in the kingdom.

The partying of Haman and Ahasuerus stands in stark contrast to what must have been the mood and mindset of the people. The callousness of the court is presented as the backdrop behind the perplexity of the people. Such pitilessness is condemned over and over in scripture.

Perhaps you've been there. You've suffered a wounding, and someone decides to poor vinegar or salt into that wound (Proverbs 25:20). Or someone celebrates when you're in trouble (Psalm 35:15).

You're not alone. Even Jesus was offered sour wine as He hung on the cross (Mark 15:23). Yet He would have you refuse to give in to despair on such occasions but remember that the callous and cruel will feel God's hand soon enough (Amos 1:11–15). Meanwhile, He will give you all the strength and hope you need to bear up under the hardship. Just wait on Him, holding fast to His love, knowing He will bless you even more in the end.

What a gift life is to those who stay the course! You've heard, of course, of Job's staying power, and you know how God brought it all together for him at the end. That's because God cares, cares right down to the last detail.

JAMES 5:11 MSG

Thank You, Lord, for giving me the strength and hope to bear up under anything that may come my way. Amen.

*Matthew Poole, *Matthew Poole's Commentary*. Text Courtesy of BibleSupport.com. Bible Hub, biblehub.com/commentaries/esther/3-15.htm

Tears Allowed

But oh! the grief of pious Mordecai!
What crushing burdens on his spirit lie. . . .
He rends his robes, and fearlessly appears
Abroad in sackcloth, clothed and bathed in tears.

When Mordecai heard about the king's new edict to kill him and all his kinsmen, he soon surmised how all this had come about, realizing that Ahasuerus had given way to the evil plotting and prompting of Haman. Overwhelmed with grief, Mordecai displayed his sorrow by ripping his garments, covering himself in sackcloth and ashes, and "crying with a loud and bitter wail" (Esther 4:1 NLT). Uttering such a loud and piercing cry was Mordecai's way of getting the attention of all the Jews in the city of Susa, that they might come to him, ask what had happened, and thus hear the news for themselves.

Rending clothing was something God's people often did to express their sadness or deep distress. Reuben did it when he learned his brothers had sold Joseph to the Midianites (Genesis 37:29). And Jacob tore at his clothes when his sons, attempting to cover up their misdeed, told him that Joseph had died (Genesis 37:34).

Putting on sackcloth and ashes, as Mordecai did, was common not only to mourning Jews but to the Persians as well. Doing so displayed the extent of their deep grief.

There's something to be said for displaying sorrow in such a demonstrative way. In many of today's societies—where people are told to buck up, to keep a stiff upper lip, to grin and bear it—our deep sadness is often swallowed down. These cultures see expressing grief as a sign of weakness.

Suffering the loss of a loved one or receiving extremely bad news is hard enough. We don't need to make it worse for ourselves or others by being told to swallow down our sorrow. The expression of grief is a critical relief valve that can clear the way to healing.

To help us get on the right side of demonstrating sorrow, we can look to the behavior of those who have gone before. Consider Abraham, who "went to mourn for Sarah and to weep for her" (Genesis 23:2 HCSB). Hannah wept (1 Samuel 1:8), much to the mystification of her husband Elkanah. David and Jonathan wept upon each other (1 Samuel 20:41). And Tamar, after her brother raped her, "tore her robe and put ashes on her head. And then, with her face in her hands, she went away crying" (2 Samuel 13:19 NLT).

Even our Lord and Master, whose example we're to follow, was filled with compassion for His friends when Lazarus died. In response, "Jesus wept" (John 11:35).

There's nothing wrong with expressing and releasing our sorrow! And as we do so, we can take comfort in the fact that in such situations, God's consolation is close.

The LORD is close to the brokenhearted;
he rescues those whose spirits are crushed.
PSALM 34:18 NLT

Come close, Lord. I need Your comfort.

Cries to Heaven

And walking Shushan's streets, he lifts on high
His prayers to God in bitter agony.
All o'er the land, in that most trying hour,
The sons of Judah fasting, wailing, pour
Their cries to Heaven, and weeping hearts o'erflow
With penitential griefs, and tears of woe.

There Mordecai sat, in the center of town in sackcloth and ashes. And there he "cried with a loud and bitter cry" (Esther 4:1 AMPC). Actually, his cry was more of a shriek, meant to attract the attention of others—and the ears and heart of God Himself.

Jews are no strangers to crying out to God. When the Egyptians were enslaving them, God's people "called out to Yahweh, the God of our fathers, and the LORD heard our cry and saw our misery, hardship, and oppression. Then the LORD brought us out of Egypt with a strong hand and an outstretched arm, with terrifying power, and with signs and wonders" (Deuteronomy 26:7–8 HCSB).

When God rescued His people from Egypt, He worked many miracles in their sight. They could actually see His power displayed, His wonders taking place before their very own eyes!

God continues to hear the prayers and cries of His people. He continues to sees what is happening in your life, your tears, your heartaches. He continues to have compassion on you. And because He loves you more than you will ever know, He will move heaven and earth to intercede on your behalf, to comfort you, to make things right, to turn evil into good. He will even work wonders on your behalf.

Yet you may not see Him move overtly, right before your eyes.

For just as He does in Esther, God will move on your behalf, but He will do so through people, events, and circumstances. He'll work through people like Mordecai and Esther. People who put Him first in their lives. People who are not afraid to come out into the open, people who are so uncaring about the opinions of others that they will clearly express. . .

- who they are: God's humble and penitent people with an expectant hope and faith.
- where they stand or sit: at His feet.
- where their power lies: in His hands and in their prayers.
- who they believe God is: a God of compassion, love, mercy, and power who hears and sees.
- what they need: Him to intercede on their behalf, to move mountains if He must.

When you need God's help, when things are so desperate that all you can do is sit before Him with tears streaming down your face, cry to Him. Make your needs known to Him. And know deep in your heart that He will move on your behalf.

No one has heard, no one has listened, no eye has seen any God except You, who acts on behalf of the one who waits for Him.
ISAIAH 64:4 HCSB

God, upon You alone I wait.

Strength amid Grief

The attendant maids and chamberlains espy,
Before the gate, the faithful Mordecai,
In sackcloth clothed, and having seen,
Report the matter to the pious queen.

When Esther was taken into the king's harem, Mordecai told her to keep her family ties, her birthplace, her ethnic background a secret (Esther 2:10). Even when she became queen, she continued to obey his direction in this regard. Thus, although some had seen and heard Mordecai inquiring about the queen's welfare (2:11) and so knew he cared about her, they knew nothing of their true relationship.

Now that same Mordecai was in the town center, weeping and wailing. He did so not only to let his people and God know of his anxiety and grief over the king's edict, but because he hoped his appearance and loud laments would attract the attention of the queen's servants. And they did. "When Queen Esther's maids and eunuchs came and told her about Mordecai, she was deeply distressed" (4:4 NLT). His behavior stirred up the compassion within Esther.

This brings to mind a woman who also needed to attract the attention of one who had the power to help her, to put an end to her suffering. Her name was Rizpah. She was a concubine of King Saul's. For five months she'd watched over the dead bodies of her two sons who were resting beside the bodies of Saul's five grandsons. They had been hung. And cursed. And now their corpses were suffering from exposure to the elements.

Rizpah spread sackcloth upon a rock, using it as a rough bed or perhaps as a tent to give her shelter while she watched over her sons' bodies, a twenty-four-hours-a-day, seven-days-a-week endeavor. "She prevented the scavenger birds from tearing at their bodies during the day and stopped wild animals from eating them at night" (2 Samuel 21:10 NLT). She was determined her boys would have a proper burial.

Eventually, Rizpah's actions were reported to David. In his mercy, David recovered the bones of Saul and Jonathan and mingled them with the bones of Rizpah's sons, burying the lot in the family grave in Zelah.

Even in our grief, God will give us the power and strength to act—and to continue to endure our hardship as well as to make progress forward. In Psalm 18:18–19 David writes, "I was in distress, but the LORD supported me. He led me to a place of safety; he rescued me because he delights in me" (NLT).

No matter how gray the present seems or how black the future appears, simply remember that God will be there for you.

You rescue the humble, but you humiliate the proud. You light
a lamp for me. The LORD, my God, lights up my darkness.
PSALM 18:27–28 NLT

Be my light, Lord, my candle in the darkness,
my balm amid the pain.

Moved to Soothe

Fair Esther, moved by sympathetic care,
To soothe his sorrows, and his burdens share,
Sent change of raiment, that her friend may wait,
With cheerful heart, within the palace gate.

a plot was in the works to wipe the Jewish population from the face of the earth. Mordecai had learned about it and had taken to shrieking in anguish while sitting in sackcloth and ashes in the center of town. He was exhibiting to one and all the sorrow and misery he felt for himself and his fellow Jews. He needed to get word to the queen.

Esther was told of Mordecai's state but not the reason for it. Extremely upset, Esther immediately moved to soothe him. But she didn't send a prominent individual of the court. She didn't send one of her ladies in waiting. She sent a nameless someone with clothes for her beloved cousin and surrogate father, charging that person to deliver them to Mordecai.

How often does God use a nameless someone to be an integral part of His plan?

One such person who comes to mind is the little servant girl who had been taken captive from Israel and brought to Syria. Rather than continually bemoaning her fate or grieving over what she once had, she applied herself to her new duties and station in life, making the best of her situation, serving Naaman's wife. Her master, Naaman, not only was a great commander for his king and a mighty man of valor, but also was a leper.

One day this little maid said to her mistress, "I wish my master would go to see the prophet in Samaria. He would heal him of his leprosy" (2 Kings 5:3 NLT).

Taking her words to heart, Naaman, with his king's permission, went to see Elisha. Eventually Naaman followed the prophet's advice to wash in the Jordan River seven times—and his skin was restored, causing Naaman to proclaim, "Now I know that there is no God in all the world except in Israel" (2 Kings 5:15 NLT)!

The Bible mentions many other nameless women of little or no power through whom God worked to further His plans, all of whom remain unknown except perhaps for where they lived or experienced God's magnificence. Consider the widow of Zarephath (1 Kings 17:8–24) or the one whose oil was multiplied (2 Kings 4:1–7). The woman of Thebez (Judges 9:53) who dropped a rock on the head of Abimelech and killed him. Pharaoh's daughter who took in baby Moses, saving the life of one who would save God's people (Exodus 2:5–10).

God can work in and through you too. Simply give Him your hands and heart. As you leave the rest up to Him, He just may use you to change the world.

"My grace is all you need. My power works best in weakness."
2 CORINTHIANS 12:9 NLT

Lord, I offer You my hands and heart. Use me as You will. Amen.

The Comforters

The robes of gladness Mordecai denies,
And wears the token of his agonies. . . .
Oh! for the power to fly on wings of love
And meet the mourner, and his sorrows prove.

Word was brought to Queen Esther that Mordecai, dressed in sackcloth, was weeping and wailing outside the King's Gate. This news brought Esther deep despair, for she didn't know the cause of her cousin's grief. So she gave a servant some clothes to take to Mordecai. Perhaps then he would come within the gate and tell her what was distressing him. But he refused her offer.

God has designed His people to want to salve the wounds of others, to give them comfort. This kind of nurturing is commonly the domain of women, who so often reach out with their hearts. God knows this very well, for He said through His prophet, "As a mother comforts her son, so I will comfort you" (Isaiah 66:13 HCSB).

Yet there will be moments when such comfort is refused or denied. Here Mordecai refused Esther's comfort of clothes. Job, himself in dire straits through no fault of his own, asked the "friends" who had come to be with him, "How do you expect me to get any comfort from your nonsense? Your so-called comfort is a tissue of lies" (Job 21:34 MSG). In both situations, the comfort offered was not enough to lift or soothe the person's spirit.

The psalmist Asaph cried aloud to God, certain God would hear him (Psalm 77:1). Yet he then writes, "In the day of my trouble I seek (inquire of and desperately require) the Lord; in the night my hand is stretched out [in prayer] without slacking up; I refuse to be comforted" (verse 2 AMPC). Why would anyone have such an attitude? Charles Spurgeon offered this suggestion: "He may have a great spiritual sorrow, and someone, who does not at all understand his grief, may proffer to him *a consolation which is far too slight*. Not knowing how deep the wound is, this foolish physician may think that it can be healed with any common ointment."*

So what is a woman to do when her salve offered for a loved one's wound is not accepted? Once she gets over the disappointment felt upon the refusal of her comfort, perhaps she may offer one soft yet clear statement: "Tell me why you are troubled, if you will, and I will listen. I am here for you, whatever you decide." Perhaps such a sentiment, offered as a promise from the truest of hearts, will be enough for the person to open up to her.

That is the course Esther took. And that is the course you too can take, along with prayer to the greatest Comforter of all.

God is. . .the source of all comfort.
2 CORINTHIANS 1:3 NLT

Lord, help me comfort others as You have so often comforted me. In Jesus' name, amen.

*Charles H. Spurgeon, "Refusing to Be Comforted," sermon, March 18, 1883, https://www.spurgeon.org/resource-library/sermons/refusing-to-be-comforted /#flipbook/.

Trusted Messengers

*A chosen chamberlain is charged to bear
Her tender message to her kindred's ear,
And strict inquiries make, that she may know
The cause of Mordecai's excessive woe.*

Esther, whose family background and relations are still under wraps, must now choose someone to carry a message to her cousin Mordecai. Who can she trust with such a delicate mission?

She selects Hathach, one of "the king's eunuchs, whom the king had appointed to attend her" (Esther 4:5 NASB). Imagine how much Esther must have trusted Hathach, who was, perhaps, her only ally within the palace. Perhaps over the five years during which she had been queen, she had grown to rely on his discretion. And now she would need to trust him even more.

We all need someone in our lives whom we can trust. Someone who will keep our deepest and darkest secrets. Someone—family member, friend, or fellow follower—who will remain true to us no matter what the cost.

Jochebed trusted her daughter Miriam with the life of her newborn son, Moses. After setting him in the weeds of the Nile, Jochebed sent Miriam to watch over her little brother. When Pharaoh's daughter came down to the river to bathe and saw Moses' little ark, she sent her maid to fetch it and discovered a beautiful baby inside. That's when Miriam stepped in and suggested that she find a Hebrew woman (her mother) to nurse him. And her offer was accepted (Exodus 2:7–10).

Another trusted messenger, who remains nameless, is known only as a "servant girl" (2 Samuel 17:17 HCSB). She relayed messages from spies at Absalom's camp to David's friends, who would tell King David what his rebellious son was up to (2 Samuel 17:17–19).

Yet there was an even more prominent messenger. Her name was Mary Magdalene. Having gone to Jesus' tomb early in the morning, she stood outside crying when two angels told her that Jesus had risen, just as He'd said. Yet she continued to cry, wanting to know where His body was. That's when Jesus appeared and spoke her name, and she recognized Him as her one and only Lord.

Trusting her to faithfully carry out His command, Jesus told her, "Don't cling to me, for I have not yet ascended to the Father. Go to my brothers and tell them, 'I ascend to my Father and your Father, my God and your God' " (John 20:17 MSG). And she did, running to the disciples and telling them all Jesus had charged her to say.

We all need people we can trust to hold our secrets, true friends who can be our allies and messengers, friends who love us and will stick with us no matter what life brings our way.

*Friends come and friends go, but a
true friend sticks by you like family.*
PROVERBS 18:24 MSG

Thank You, Lord, for good and true friends.

Cause and Effect

"Go tell the queen how Hammedatha's son,
Proud Haman, sits beside the royal throne,
Receiving reverence by the king's decree,
And Mordecai refused to bow the knee."

Esther's attendant Hathach proceeded to obey his mistress's command to speak with Mordecai, who was wearing sackcloth and sitting in ashes in the open square of the city. The servant's mission was to discover what had brought the Jew to wailing and weeping for all the world to see.

Here we must pause and consider what had to be going through Mordecai's mind when he told his story to Hathach. For he had to begin at the beginning (Esther 4:7), meaning that the catalyst that had brought all this about was Mordecai's refusal to bow to Haman. Had Mordecai not been determined to follow the way of God by refusing to pay homage to a mere mortal—and such a despicable mortal as Haman—none of this would have happened! *Gill's Exposition of the Bible* puts it this way: "And Mordecai told him of all that had happened unto him. . . . How that, for refusing to reverence Haman, he was incensed against him, and against all the Jews for his sake; and had vowed revenge on them, and had formed a scheme for the ruin of them."*

And now, because of Mordecai's actions, because of his reverence for God alone, he was going to have to ask his surrogate daughter to risk her life to save their people! How much worse could this situation get?

Mordecai knew of God's promises. He knew that if he lived his life in obedience to God, he would prosper and be blessed for doing the right thing (Deuteronomy 5:33; Proverbs 11:18). But right now, as he sat in sackcloth and ashes, he might not have felt blessed at all.

Perhaps you have experienced the same thing as our friend Mordecai. You were minding your own business and someone came along and caused you trouble. You responded the right way, did the right thing, the thing God had told you to do, but then you and perhaps others suffered from it (Exodus 5:20–21).

It's during times like these we must remember that walking with God doesn't mean we will never have heartaches or go through turbulent times. But what it does mean is that God will be with us as we go through them.

Our mission is to follow God, to follow His way, and to walk in the Spirit no matter what consequences we may suffer in the flesh. Then, when those big but perhaps unpopular decisions have to be made, God will give us the strength to stand firm in Him and find His peace in the process.

He's a. . .personal bodyguard to the candid and sincere.
He keeps his eye on all who live honestly, and pays
special attention to his loyally committed ones.
PROVERBS 2:7–8 MSG

Stand with me, Lord, as I stand firm in You.

*John Gill, *John Gill's Exposition of the Bible*. Text Courtesy of Internet Sacred Texts Archive. biblehub.com/commentaries/esther/4-7.htm

The Price of Palatability

"Tell how the oppressor gained the king's command
To slay the Jews who dwell in every land;
And promised, when the deed was done, to bring
Ten thousand talents to enrich the king."

O bedient to his mistress Queen Esther, Hathach asked Mordecai why he was sitting in front of the King's Gate wearing sackcloth and sitting in ashes. We can imagine Mordecai, speaking in clear but perhaps whispered tones to his daughter's faithful servant, explaining exactly what had happened. To do so, Mordecai had to go back to the beginning.

Because Mordecai had refused to bow to Haman, the miscreant had resolved to kill not just Mordecai but all Jews. To make such a scheme palatable to King Ahasuerus, Haman offered to pay 10,000 talents into the king's treasury (Esther 3:9) for an edict allowing him to do so (4:7).

There is some discrepancy among Bible scholars as to whether Ahasuerus actually accepted such a bribe. For when the king was first offered the money, he said, "The money and the people are both yours to do with as you see fit" (3:11 NLT). This statement could be seen as the king's refusal or perhaps was just a polite way of expressing his acceptance while simultaneously appearing magnanimous (similar to the situation between Ephron and Abraham when they haggled over the price of some real estate [Genesis 23:11–15]). Either way, Esther later brings up this side of the plot to the king, telling him her people were "*sold out* to destruction, death, and extermination" (Esther 7:4 HCSB, emphasis added).

Regardless of whether Ahasuerus accepted the bribe, Haman's

offering of it shows the seriousness of his intention to wipe out an entire race of people to soothe his wounded pride. And it indicates that money was used to make the plan more palatable to the king.

Such information would have been alarming to Esther, perhaps causing her to wonder if her husband would be cursed for accepting such a bribe (Deuteronomy 27:25). At the very least, it may have brought to mind the warning found in Exodus 23:8: "Take no bribes, for a bribe makes you ignore something that you clearly see. A bribe makes even a righteous person twist the truth" (NLT). Wherever this information may have led Esther's thoughts, one thing is clear: God detests the one who offers a bribe as well as the one who accepts it.

If you're ever in a position where someone offers you money or goods so you will more clearly "see things their way," stop. Lift up your thoughts to God. Consider what that person is really asking you. And consider your next steps. Those who take bribes become blind to truth and justice—and the innocent are the ones who are harmed in the end.

> *Make sure that your character is free from the*
> *love of money, being content with what you have.*
> HEBREWS 13:5 NASB

Lord, may I be content in You alone.

Mansplaining?

"Go show this bloody scroll that sets the day,
Not sparing age, or sex, or rank, to slay
The Jewish race, and all their substance hold,
The soldiers' portion, and the spoilers' gold."

When we first read Esther 4:8, Mordecai seems to want the servant Hathach to "mansplain" to Esther the king's edict to annihilate the Jewish people. For the text reads, "[Mordecai] also gave him a copy of the decree to destroy them, that was given out in Shushan, that he might show it to Esther, *explain it to her*, and charge her to go to the king, make supplication to him, and plead with him for the lives of her people" (Esther 4:8 AMPC, emphasis added). But this could also mean Mordecai simply wanted the direness of the situation to be stressed to Esther so she would realize its consequences for the future of God's people.

It's easy for a woman to get her nose out of joint when men are advising her. She has to ascertain if she's getting solid advice or if her intelligence is being ignored or her ideas brushed aside.

The word *mansplaining* was added to the Oxford English Dictionary in 2018. Its definition is "Of a man: to explain (something) needlessly, overbearingly, or condescendingly, esp. (typically when addressing a woman) in a manner thought to reveal a patronizing or chauvinistic attitude."

It may behoove us to consider here if the male characters within this text believe Esther does indeed need mansplaining. Perhaps those who were blinded by her beauty could not see beyond her pretty face and thus missed the mind behind it.

As her surrogate father, Mordecai must have known his adopted daughter well. He'd likely taught her who God is and how His people had been dispersed to live among pagans. Thus, he must have known her level of intelligence.

But at this point in our story, Esther had been queen for five years. Before that she'd been living away from home, residing in the king's harem for at least one year. So for six years Esther and Mordecai had been away from each other. The only news he'd had about her had been gleaned from his inquiries to palace servants. Perhaps he thought she'd "dumbed down."

Whether Mordecai urged a servant to mansplain things to his queen may be irrelevant. We should focus more on the words of Esther and the character she displays than on the opinions and words of the men within her story. For in her words and actions we will find the proof of her courage, intelligence, wisdom, and dedication to her God and people. No mansplaining necessary.

> *A capable, intelligent, and virtuous woman—who is he who can find her? She is far more precious than jewels and her value is far above rubies or pearls.*
>
> PROVERBS 31:10 AMPC

Help me, Lord, to become the wise and courageous woman You created me to be. Amen.

There Is a Time

"Go charge the queen before the king t' appear,
And pour her melting, supplicating prayer
To change the sovereign's will, and lead the king
To grant relief, and to her people safety bring."

Hathach now knew the backstory behind Haman's evil edict and the king's support of it. Revenge had been sought. Money exchanged. The proclamation sent out. The edict itself was in Hathach's hands.

And now Mordecai instructed the servant to show the decree to Esther. To make sure she understood the peril to the Jewish people. Then, hoping to God he could trust the eunuch, Mordecai told Hathach to urge Esther to "go to the king, make supplication to him, and plead with him for the lives of *her* people" (Esther 4:8 AMPC, emphasis added). And the proverbial cat was out of the bag.

Mordecai had taken the risk of sharing another's secret, but he had no way of knowing what would come of it.

Let's face it. We all have secrets—those of our own and sometimes those of others. And often we come to a crossroad in life when those secrets must be shared for the good of all. But how do we determine when, where, and to whom the confidences of others should be revealed?

The book of Proverbs has a lot to say about secrets. It describes those who keep secrets as trustworthy and people of integrity (11:13). It says that gossips and bigmouths reveal secrets (20:19); that if you guard your mouth as well as your tongue, you'll stay out of trouble (21:23); and that even if you're arguing with someone, you shouldn't reveal her secret—if you do, no one will trust you afterward (25:9–10).

Micah tells us that we shouldn't trust anyone with a confidence—neither neighbor nor friend; that we at all times should just keep our mouths shut (Micah 7:5). Even Jesus said we should safeguard secrets (Matthew 9:28–30; 16:19–20). At the same time, God knows the secrets of our hearts (Psalm 44:21). He knows everything about everyone. He knows when we sit down, when we go out, and when we get angry with Him (2 Kings 19:27). Yet if we call to Him, He'll tell us things—secret, hidden, wondrous things (Jeremiah 33:3).

We need to remember that every secret eventually comes out (Ecclesiastes 10:20; Matthew 10:26; Mark 4:22; Luke 12:2; 8:17). That there is "a time to be silent and a time to speak" (Ecclesiastes 3:7 HCSB), especially when we need to speak up for those who cannot speak for themselves (Proverbs 31:8). The best course of action is to go to God and ask Him for advice. He'll help you decide whether to release the cat or hold fast to its tail.

*If you need wisdom, ask our generous God, and he
will give it to you. He will not rebuke you for asking.*
JAMES 1:5 NLT

---

*Lord, give me discernment to know when
to speak and when to remain silent.*

A Reluctant Heroine

The appointed messenger makes haste to bear
The thrilling news to Esther's waiting ear;
And quick brings back the anxious queen's reply,
That wakes anew the griefs of Mordecai.

In Esther 4:9–10 we are given two short pieces of information—actions, actually. The first is that the faithful servant Hathach brought the edict to Esther and told her everything Mordecai had said. The second is that Esther gave Hathach a reply to relay back to Mordecai. And the reply was that of a somewhat reluctant heroine.

Esther was obviously disquieted, for she knew the danger that lay ahead of her. And soon Mordecai would know the cause of her fears. This would then awaken in him the desire to protect his young and beloved cousin. At the same time, he knew that Esther had a pivotal role to play in the salvation of their people.

The reluctant hero is an archetype often found in fiction. It's someone who shuffles her feet a bit, perhaps trying to work up the courage to forge ahead into the unknown and often perilous situation that will have monumental consequences for her future. She may need some coaxing only in the beginning of the story. But sometimes she needs encouragement all along the way.

We've met such reluctant heroes before. Moses gave God several reasons he wasn't the man for God's job (Exodus 3–4). Barak, although encouraged to lead the Israelites against Sisera, wouldn't go without Deborah. She warned him, "I will go with you. . .but you will receive no honor on the road you are about to take, because the Lord will sell Sisera into a woman's hand" (Judges 4:9 HCSB). While in hiding, Gideon also made excuses to God when God called him to lead His people (Judges 6).

About Esther, F. B. Meyer writes,

> *In reply to the demand that she should hazard
> her life for the people, there was at first a natural
> reluctance. Was her love for her people greater than
> her love for herself? In her resolve there was surely
> something of the great love of Christ. We may be
> quite sure that God will carry out His plans—with
> us, if possible; if not, in spite of us, to our utter
> loss. We should look upon our position as a sacred
> trust to be used for others. We are created for good
> works, which God hath prepared for us to walk in.
> There can be no presumption in action which is
> preceded by prayer and heart-searching.*

When you have an opportunity to be a heroine, may you, like
Esther. . .

> *Trust in the LORD with all your heart; do not depend on
> your own understanding. Seek his will in all you do,
> and he will show you which path to take.*
> PROVERBS 3:5–6 NLT

Dear Lord, may I become the heroine You created me to be.

Invitation Only

*"No one on pain of death may e'er resort
To meet the king within the inner court;
When venturing there uncalled, life trembling stands
As waves the scepter in the sovereign's hands."*

Mordecai told Esther she should approach the king and plead for her people. Sounds easy enough. Yet there was a sticking point to this venture. A law known by all court officials and the general population decreed, "Anyone who appears before the king in his inner court without being invited is doomed to die unless the king holds out his gold scepter" (Esther 4:11 NLT).

And there was a good reason behind this law. There had been many political assassinations in the land. Also, the king had to maintain the dignity of his person. Not just anyone could be allowed to approach him. So even though Esther was the *queen*, the favored wife of Ahasuerus, she trembled at the thought of approaching him uninvited.

Thank God Jesus gives us access to God's throne of grace, allowing us to "with confidence draw near. . .that we may receive mercy and find grace to help in time of need" (Hebrews 4:16 ESV). Because of Jesus, we don't have to wait until God calls us to approach Him. We can go to Him knowing He won't turn away from us but rather turn toward us to hear our prayer, give us advice, and guide us to the right path.

And even if we don't know what to say, even if we cannot find the words, the questions, the thoughts that are plaguing our minds, we have the Holy Spirit to help translate what we cannot put into words (Romans 8:26–27).

Only Jesus can give us the courage we need to bring our prayers and petitions before God's majestic throne, as well as the patience we may need as we wait for His answer.

Matthew Henry writes:

> *We are prone to shrink from services that are attended with peril or loss. But when the cause of Christ and his people demand it, we must take up our cross, and follow him. When Christians are disposed to consult their own ease or safety, rather than the public good, they should be blamed. The law was express, all knew it. It is not thus in the court of the King of kings: to the footstool of his throne of grace we may always come boldly, and may be sure of an answer of peace to the prayer of faith. We are welcome, even into the holiest, through the blood of Jesus.**

Today if you have something to ask God or put before Him, don't avoid it. Don't stand there trembling. Instead, approach boldly, knowing He will hear and He will help.

> *Walk right up to him and get what he is so ready to give. Take the mercy, accept the help.*
> HEBREWS 4:16 MSG

Here I am, Lord. Let's talk.

*Matthew Henry, *Concise Commentary on the Whole Bible*, https://biblehub.com/commentaries/esther/4-11.htm

Hope amid Uncertainty

*"No call for thirty days has come to me,
To stand before the royal majesty;
A gleam of hope alone have I to place
My life upon the king's uncertain grace."*

*E*sther not only faced the peril of death by going before the king uninvited but also may have fallen out of his favor. It had been thirty days since she had last seen the king. Perhaps he had tired of her. Or found a young girl more willing, more beautiful, more Persian. All Esther had was a bit of hope that if she approached the king without being called, her life would be spared by his "uncertain grace."

Perhaps there were even more uncertainties facing Esther. Perhaps she wondered if these messages being sent back and forth through her servant Hathach were being translated with the appropriate inflection or if any words were being lost between the palace and Malachi's place outside the king's gate.

It's hard to know what to do when our minds are filled with a mountain of what-ifs. We become immobile, unable to make a decision. When our tide of confidence has ebbed, we begin thinking wild thoughts.

Perhaps you have been in such a place. Your insecurities have taken over your mind, have caused your courage to begin to wane. You begin to wonder if you're called, worthy, chosen, beautiful, or special enough—to anyone, including God!

The answer is yes. And here's why.

You are God's masterpiece. You have been created in Christ Jesus to do some amazing things, which God prepared in advance for you to do (Ephesians 2:10). You are the work of the hands of the King of Kings (Isaiah 64:8). God lives within you and will help you to stand (Psalm 46:5). You can be not just strong but courageous—because God has commanded you to be so and because God walks with you (Joshua 1:9). You will be blessed when you believe that God will fulfill His promises to you (Luke 1:45)!

And no need to worry about your beauty on the outside. Because what's important is your *inner* self, that "beauty that comes from within, the unfading beauty of a gentle and quiet spirit, which is so precious to God" (1 Peter 3:4 NLT).

When you start to doubt you are enough, remember how precious you are in God's eyes (Isaiah 43:4), how much He not just loves you but rejoices over you (Zephaniah 3:17), how much He values you (Luke 12:6–7), and how you will never ever walk alone (Deuteronomy 31:8).

God promises you all these things (Deuteronomy 7:9). So don't worry about anything but go to God with everything (Philippians 4:6), firmly believing in His goodness.

I will see the LORD's goodness in the land of the living. Wait for the LORD; be strong and courageous. Wait for the LORD.
PSALM 27:13–14 HCSB

Thank You, Lord, for transforming my uncertainty to hope and my angst to courage. Amen.

The Hiding Place

"Think not within the royal house to stand,
When the wild judgment passes o'er the land.
The sword that seeks the blood of all our race
Will find the queen within her hiding place."

Esther's messages—that her life would be in jeopardy if she went to the king without an invitation and that she hadn't seen him for a month—had been relayed to Mordecai. Rather than considering the reasons for her hesitancy, Mordecai quickly got to the heart of the matter: what could happen if she did *not* try to intercede on behalf of the Jewish people.

The picture Mordecai painted was not pretty. He told his adopted daughter that if she did nothing, there was every chance in the world that she, along with her countrymen and -women, would be among those killed under Haman's evil edict. In other words, her connections to the royals likely wouldn't be enough to protect her, no matter where she hid.

When we attempt to ignore the problems of others, to avoid speaking up for or taking action on behalf of people who are being abused by society or government, we take the risk of being injured ourselves. Yet denial of our own responsibility comes at a cost.

Consider Abigail. When she heard of how her husband Nabal had been insolent to David and his men, refusing supplies to those who had been a wall of protection around Nabal's shepherds, she knew trouble was on its way. So Abigail "wasted no time" (1 Samuel 25:18 NLT) in gathering supplies and meeting with David face-to-face. If she had tried to hide, all would have been lost. Instead, she not only saved her people but later became David's wife.

Next, consider Jehosheba. When Athalia, mother of the late King Ahaziah, decided to annihilate his heirs to Judean throne, Ahaziah's half sister Jehosheba stole away "Ahaziah's infant son, Joash. . .from among the rest of the king's children, who were about to be killed. She. . .hid him from Athaliah" (2 Kings 11:2 NLT), thus saving the life of the future king.

Finally, consider Barak, the commander of Israel's army, who refused go into battle against Sisera, the commander of King Jabin of Canaan, and his men unless Deborah went with him. Because he basically wanted to hide behind Deborah's courage, the glory of the eventual victory went not to Barak but to a woman, just as Deborah had prophesied (Judges 4:9).

We cannot hide from the injustices of this world no matter how great our connections to the influential and powerful. Instead, we must stand up for others against evildoers (Psalm 94:16), knowing God will give us the courage and clear heads to do so.

In the multitude of my [anxious] thoughts within me,
Your comforts cheer and delight my soul!
PSALM 94:19 AMPC

Give me the strength, courage, protection,
and clear head I need as I stand up to the
injustices against Your people, Lord. Amen.

Holding Peace

"Should Esther hold her peace in this dark hour,
Our fathers' God, the God whom we adore,
Will stand on Judah's side, a shield and rock,
And give enlargement to his suffering flock.
And as redemption to the Jews shall rise,
Thy father's house shall fall a sacrifice. . . ."

We are to live and give our lives for others. What we have received is not for our satisfaction alone but is meant to be shared with the body of fellow believers.

When it comes to what God would have us do for others, we are to hold nothing back. If we do, we will be found out. And we're to live and give not so we can be commended by others but so we can be faithful to and commended by God.

Alexander Maclaren writes in his *Expositions*, "Whatever is not used for God becomes a snare first, then injures the possessors, and tends to destroy the possessors. The march of Providence goes on. Its purposes will be effected. Whatever stands in the way will be mowed remorselessly down, if need be. Helps that have become hindrances will go."*

Consider Ananias and his wife, Sapphira. Their story appears after we're told all new Christians began to share everything. And because they did so, not one among them was needy. "Those who owned fields or houses sold them and brought the price of the sale to the apostles and made an offering of it. The apostles then distributed it according to each person's need" (Acts 4:35–36 MSG).

Then the conniving couple Ananias and Sapphira enter the picture. They sold a piece of land and, unbeknownst to anyone but them, kept part of the proceeds for themselves. When Ananias purported to offer the full amount to the apostles, Peter understood right away what was happening, saying, "Ananias, how did Satan get you to lie to the Holy Spirit and secretly keep back part of the price of the field? Before you sold it, it was all yours, and after you sold it, the money was yours to do with as you wished. So what got into you to pull a trick like this?" (Acts 5:3–4 MSG).

After hearing Peter's words, Ananias fell down dead. Less than three hours later, Saphira showed up, hoping to propagate the same lie her husband had told. She too wound up dead. So much for that household.

Sometimes in the busyness of our days or in the worst of hardships, we forget who God made us to be: children of and believers in a God of truth who wants all of us and all we have to be dedicated to Him, nothing held back but given freely for others.

> *"As for me and my family, we will serve the LORD."*
> JOSHUA 24:15 NLT

I bring all of myself and all I have to You, Lord.
What would You have me do?

*Alexander Maclaren, *Expositions of Holy Scripture,* https://biblehub.com/commentaries/esther/4-14.htm

God Only Knows

"And who can tell but God has raised thee high
A saviour in this hour of agony!"

*E*sther and Mordecai had been having a rather protracted covert conversation, each person's point being conveyed through a servant. Finally Mordecai laid down his final and strongest argument for why Esther should put her life on the line for her fellow Jews, saying, "Who knows but that you have come to the kingdom for such a time as this and for this very occasion?" (Esther 4:14 AMPC).

This is the question each Christian woman should be asking herself.

Woman of faith, why are you in the position you are in at this point in time? What is it God may be calling you to do, say, see, learn, become? What destiny do you believe God has in mind for you?

Esther's rise to the position of queen seems unlikely at best. At an early age, she lost both her parents. As an orphan, she was adopted by her uncle Mordecai. By him, she was taught about the one and only God of the Hebrews. And she grew into a beautiful woman in a country in which her people were exiles.

Then King Ahasuerus got drunk at a party, called on his queen, was met with her disobedience, and ousted her. Subsequently, a sweep was made of the country and all beautiful young virgins were rounded up to be added to the royal harem. After various beautifying processes, each was presented to the king. Of them all, Esther was chosen to become the next queen of Persia! And now here she was, in just the right position to help prevent the annihilation of her people! Perhaps that was why all these things happened. God needed someone to do an inside job for Him. She was the only one who could do it, who could be used by God in a particular way for a particular outcome.

The same type of thing happened to Joseph. If he hadn't had dreams about being bowed down to, if his brothers hadn't been jealous, if he hadn't been sold into slavery, if he hadn't wound up in a dungeon, if he hadn't continued to trust in God, he wouldn't have been in a position to ensure the survival of God's people in Egypt.

God has a plan for each of His children. We might not know exactly what that plan is, but we don't really need to. All we need to do is trust in the One who has designed this earth, its denizens, and our destiny. To be curious each day as to why God has put us here at this particular time. To believe that what He calls us to do He will help us do in every hour and situation.

"It wasn't you who sent me here but God. He set me in place."
GENESIS 45:7 MSG

Lord, what would You have me do at this time in this place?

The Prevailing Advocate

The advocate prevails. Fair Esther yearns
For Judah's good, and thus her word returns.

Esther had put all her concerns out there to Mordecai. She'd mulled over the situation. And she'd made a decision.

Yet why did it take her so long? What was the problem? Why couldn't she clearly see what she should do?

Men and women go through a different process when trying to make a decision. Women are long-distance runners. They take their time, investigating various options. They begin by collecting information, asking others for their thoughts and opinions. Only after weighing and processing that information do they make up their minds. Men, on the other hand, sprint for the finish line.

Each method has its drawbacks. As a woman explores factors a man might not even consider, she may take umbrage to his quick answer. At the same time, a man may get impatient, wondering why the woman can't just make up her mind.

Fortunately, we have a go-between in situations where difficult decisions need to be made: the Holy Spirit. The New Testament calls Him the Helper or Advocate.

The Holy Spirit has been around since the very beginning, hovering above the waters of chaos (Genesis 1:1–2). He came upon people who needed help, giving them insight into their circumstances, as well as other powers. A dying King David talked about Him, saying, "The Spirit of the Lord spoke in and by me" (2 Samuel 23:2 AMPC). The Spirit even led David in the ways of God (Psalm 143:10).

And the Spirit did not speak to men alone. He also spoke to

women such as Miriam, sister to Aaron and Moses (Micah 6:4). He spoke to a woman with no nomenclatures other than Samson's mother and Manoah's wife, revealing to her God's plan through her soon-to-be-born son (Judges 13). Speaking through the Angel or Man of God, God was totally trusting this woman to obey His instructions without her husband's help, hand, permission, or voice in the matter. Even King Lemuel's mother passed on some words to her son, wisdom she had been given by God (Proverbs 31:1–9).

Thus, we can safely infer that Esther had called upon the Spirit of God to come to her as her Helper and Advocate. To come alongside her, giving her the both the wisdom and the courage to accept the challenge put before her.

When you are searching for God's particular purpose or plan for you at any time in your life, begin with the Spirit. Ask Him to help you find your way; to give you the wisdom you need. Then open yourself up to His guidance, knowing that when you do. . .

Your ears will hear a word behind you, saying, "This is the way, walk in it," whenever you turn to the right or to the left.
ISAIAH 30:21 NASB

Spirit, speak to my heart. Fill me with the wisdom I need.

Esther's Transformation

"Go gather all the Jews who now are found,
Mourning within the royal city's bound
And keep a fast for me. Three days and nights
In strictest form observe the solemn rites."

Esther, having made her decision, proceeded to put a plan in motion. She sent a message to Mordecai, saying, "Go and assemble all the Jews who can be found in Susa and fast for me. Don't eat or drink for three days, day or night. I and my female servants will also fast in the same way" (Esther 4:16 HCSB). The young girl who became queen now seems to have transformed into a determined and confident woman of God!

In the beginning of Esther's story, we see her as an orphan cut off not only from her parents but, as an exiled Jew living in Persia, from her nation as well. Fortunately, her cousin Mordecai, able and willing to step into the breach, raised her as his own daughter and taught her of the God of Israel.

The next transition for Esther was being taken from her home with Mordecai and into a harem. His parting warning was to keep her family ties and nationality a secret. He basically advised her to try to blend in.

We then see Esther taking the advice of Hegai, the chief eunuch in charge of the harem, who had taken a fancy to her. He gave her tips on wardrobe, beauty treatments, and diet.

A year or so later, she was accepted by the king as the next queen. Even then, "Esther still had not revealed her birthplace or her ethnic background, as Mordecai had directed. She obeyed

Mordecai's orders, as she always had while he raised her" (Esther 2:20 HCSB).

Now, finding out about the king's edict to destroy their countrymen, Mordecai advised Esther once more, telling her she must stand up for her people.

After considering the danger in this endeavor, Esther came up with a firm directive for Mordecai. She told him to gather all the Jews in the city in mourning and hold a strict three-day fast. The daughter wasn't just advising her surrogate father but commanding him. And "Mordecai went and did everything Esther had ordered him" (Esther 4:17 HCSB).

There comes a time in every woman's life when she, although respectful of her parents, becomes the main decision maker. Although still a child to aging parents, she is now directing her own life and, at times, theirs.

The only parent a young girl will never outgrow is her heavenly Father. For she will ever remain the young child of her Abba. And it is His advice alone she determines to follow.

Listen for GOD's voice in everything you do,
everywhere you go; he's the one who will keep
you on track. . . . A father's delight is behind all this.
PROVERBS 3:6, 12 MSG

Lead my life, Abba God. Your child is ready.

Prayer Moves

"And keep a fast for me. Three days and nights
In strictest form observe the solemn rites.
I and my maids will keep the holy fast;
And when the days of tears and prayers are passed. . ."

*E*sther knew and believed in the power of prayer. For in her message to Mordecai, she asked him to have the Jews pray and fast for her for three days and nights, employing the "strictest form" amid the solemn rites.

This queen was no fool. Prayer *is* one of our most powerful tools. Time and time again it has altered the course of events in earthly and spiritual realms. Charles H. Spurgeon said, "Prayer bends the omnipotence of heaven to your desire. Prayer moves the hands that move the world."*

Although the name of God is not mentioned in this passage—nor in the entire book of Esther—it is clear that God's wisdom, power, strength, and courage were what the Jews were seeking. And, according to the Word, they would find the provision they needed. For James 5:16 tells us, "Make this your common practice: Confess your sins to each other and pray for each other so that you can live together whole and healed. The prayer of a person living right with God is something powerful to be reckoned with" (MSG).

James goes on to tell us of the time Elijah "prayed hard that it wouldn't rain, and it didn't—not a drop for three and a half years. Then he prayed that it would rain, and it did. The showers came and everything started growing again" (James 5:17–18 MSG).

When he was thrown in the lions' den, Daniel prayed to God to rescue him. So God sent His angel to shut the mouths of the lions so that Daniel would emerge from his ordeal unscathed (Daniel 6:19–22). When King Hezekiah received his death notice from God via Isaiah, he prayed for God to extend his life, and God did (Isaiah 38).

Yet Esther hadn't just asked Mordecai to organize the Jews to pray. She also asked him to have them fast—for three days and three nights. Why? So that their prayers would be focused, concentrated. In fasting, they would more clearly hear the direction and guidance of God. Prolonged fasting also demonstrated the depth of their devotion and the seriousness of their desire to see God move.

Perhaps something is happening in your own life, some risk you feel you may have to take, or a somewhat perilous endeavor that will require not just a leap of your faith but a concentrated time of prayer and fasting. If so, follow Esther's example. Ask others to fast and pray for you, remembering that "sometimes, all it takes is just one prayer to change everything."†

> *We fasted and pleaded with our God. . .*
> *and He granted our request.*
> Ezra 8:23 hcsb

Lord, today I come to You upon my knees. Hear my prayer.

*Charles H. Spurgeon.
†Source of quotation unknown.

Spirits Cling

*"When God is honored, and our spirits cling
To one who sits above the Persian king,
Uncalled, unguarded, and alone, I'll stand
And trust the scepter in the sovereign's hand."*

*A*fter commanding Mordecai to gather all the Jews to hold a three-day prayer-and-fasting vigil for her, which she and her female servants also would partake in, Esther told him she would go to the king without being summoned, which was against the law in the kingdom of Persia. She would risk her life on behalf of her people.

How did she gain such courage, such coolness of mind? By honoring God. By allowing no barrier between herself and her God.

Something amazing happens when we praise our God. Untold heavenly powers are released to assist us. By paying tribute to our Father, we remember He is the One truly in control, the One who rules over not just us but all people—kings, queens, presidents, prime ministers, everyone!

As we focus on Him, we realize that God alone is the One we need. That our only role is to do as He bids, walk as He wills. To find the strength and power to accomplish our part in God's plan, our spirits are to cling to His. Moses tells us, "You shall walk after the LORD your God and you shall fear [and worship] Him [with awe-filled reverence and profound respect], and you shall keep His commandments and you shall listen to His voice, and you shall serve Him, and cling to Him" (Deuteronomy 13:4 AMP).

In his farewell address to God's people, Joshua reinforced this idea, telling the people, "Cling to the LORD your God, just as you have done to this day" (Joshua 23:8 AMP).

While David was in the wilderness, he told God that he thought of God when he was lying in bed at night because God was his helper. He rejoiced in God because God had always been there for him. He said, "My soul [my life, my very self] clings to You; Your right hand upholds me" (Psalm 63:8 AMP). Why should we cling to God? Because when we do, He will hold us as "steady as a post" (Psalm 63:8 MSG).

God knows we need calm, courage, and strength in the direst of situations. That's why He wants us to know He is there for us every step of the way. But to ensure His closeness to use, we must get close to Him. James 4:8 tells us, "Draw near to God, and He will draw near to you" (HCSB).

So cling to the One who calls you (Isaiah 49:1), who guards and goes before you (Isaiah 52:12). Allow Him not only to ease your stress with His calm (Zephaniah 3:17) but to be right beside you as you face all earthly powers.

> *Trust and take refuge in the LORD! [Be confident*
> *in Him, cling to Him, rely on His word!]*
> PSALM 115:9 AMP

Lord, to You alone my spirit clings!

Perish the Thought

"And if I perish, thro' my country's laws,
I'll perish in my people's righteous cause."

Two of the most recognized verses from the book of Esther come in chapter 4. The first one is said by Mordecai to Esther: "Who knows but that you have come to the kingdom for such a time as this?" (verse 14 AMPC). The second is said by Esther to Mordecai: "And if I perish, I perish" (verse 16 AMPC).

Here we realize the commitment Esther had finally made—to her uncle, her people, and herself. She, although a queen, faced death by going to her husband without an invitation. And all to gain his ear on behalf of her people who themselves were facing imminent death.

Such a sentiment as "If I perish, I perish" was expressed another time by three young men—Shadrach, Meshach, and Abednego—when they refused to bow down to King Nebuchadnezzar's golden idol. Their punishment was to be thrown into a blazing hot furnace. In response, they told Nebuchadnezzar, "If you throw us in the fire, the God we serve can rescue us from your roaring furnace. . . . But even if he doesn't, it wouldn't make a bit of difference, O king. We still wouldn't serve your gods or worship the gold statue you set up" (Daniel 3:17–18 MSG).

Interestingly enough, both Esther and these three young men were coming face-to-face with death as a result of refusing to go against their God and worship someone other than Him. They committed themselves to doing the right thing in God's eyes, to taking the plunge, leaping in faith, and refusing to turn back, knowing very well what the consequences of their actions might be.

When a cause is righteous, when your path is the only one a godly person can take, all that is left for you is to do the right thing and leave the rest to God. To relax in the truth that no matter what happens to you on this earth, no matter what arrows and slings of misfortune are aimed at you, you are on the right road with God. And to know, in the end, that's all that really matters.

In the eyes of unbelievers, your taking God's side in any situation may seem foolish. When you are powerless and decide to stand up against the powerful, others may mock you, tell you you're an idiot, talk about you behind your back. But like Esther and others, you know the truth. That "God has chosen the foolish things of the world to shame the wise, and God has chosen the weak things of the world to shame the things which are strong" (1 Corinthians 1:27 NASB). Grounding yourself in this truth while keeping your eyes on God is what will enable you to stand up for those who cannot stand up for themselves.

Trust not in human wisdom but in the power of God.
1 CORINTHIANS 2:5 NLT

Lord, give me the confidence to trust in
Your power, not the wisdom of men.

Heavenly Address

The queen has clothed her soul in heavenly dress,
In robes of faith, and hope, and holiness;
Has brightened all her gems of grace that shine
Inimitable, pure, like things divine.

Esther had fasted for three days and nights, focusing on her soul. She had prayed and prayed for God to lend her His ear, to allow her to partake of His guidance, courage, strength, and power.

As she did so, He clothed her in robes of faith. He increased her hope. He transformed her spirit of fear and fainting into a spirit of bravery and determination (see Isaiah 61:3). He equipped her with what she needed so she could do what He'd called her to do, shining bright in "the armor of light" (Romans 13:12 NASB).

When we know we will soon face a nerve-wracking, perhaps even life-jeopardizing situation, we must remember to spend time in God's presence beforehand, truly seeking—with all our heart, soul, and mind—His face, strength, protection, and wisdom. We need to refocus our entire being on God, trusting in His power—not our own—to rule the day.

When he heard that powerful armies were heading his way, King Jehoshaphat "was terrified. . .and begged the LORD for guidance. He also ordered everyone in Judah to begin fasting" (2 Chronicles 20:3 NLT). People from all over came to Jerusalem to seek God's help. Jehoshaphat's prayer helped himself and his people to refocus on who God is and where their power lay:

> *"O LORD, God of our fathers. . .power and might are*
> *in Your hand, there is no one able to take a stand*

against You. . . . We are powerless against this
great multitude which is coming against us. We do
not know what to do, but our eyes are on You."
(2 Chronicles 20:6, 12 AMP)

Jehoshaphat and his people knew that whenever they were "faced with any calamity" (2 Chronicles 20:9 NLT), they could cry out to God to save them. That He would then hear and rescue them.

While in captivity, Nehemiah, serving as cupbearer to an earlier Persian king, heard about Jerusalem's broken walls and fire-ravaged gates. He too began to fast and pray. He admitted to God that His people had sinned by not following His ways. When Nehemiah planned to approach King Artaxerxes to ask him to help God's people, the cupbearer humbled himself before God and prayed, "Please grant me success today by making the king favorable to me" (Nehemiah 1:11 NLT).

On his way back to Jerusalem with some exiled Jews, Ezra proclaimed a fast, "so that we might humble ourselves before our God and ask Him for a safe journey" (Ezra 8:21 HCSB).

Because of each person's prayer and fasting, because of their dedication to and focus on God alone, He not only clothed them in faith, increased their hope, transformed their fear to courage, and equipped them for their task, but gave them success. If you follow their example, He will do the same for you.

"We are powerless. . .but our eyes are on You."
2 Chronicles 20:12 AMP

Lord, I don't know what to do, but my eyes are on You.

Radiating Calm

'Twas just the hour of evening sacrifice,
When Judah's prayers and incense reached the skies;
When Esther, heaven-supported, passed the door.
Her face was radiant, while her heart was sore,
And stood before the throne, calm and serene,
The peerless beauty, and the enchanting queen.

For three days and three nights Esther and her people had prayed and fasted. Now, in this moment of time, she walked alone toward the most powerful man in the kingdom. And she did so not knowing if or how far she had fallen out of favor with him.

Her faith underlying her courage, Esther, girded by God's power, walked toward the throne of her king, lord, master, husband. She did so at the same time the prayers of her people were wending their way up (Psalm 141:2; Revelation 8:4) to their heavenly King, the One who stood high above this earthly king sitting on his ivory throne.

Fortified by her people's faith as well as her own, Esther stood before her king (Esther 5:1), her face radiating the peace of God's presence, her manner exuding serenity and grace. How beautiful she must have been to behold as she offered her own life, reckless in her love for her people, sensing that as she put her earthly life in God's hands, she would somehow live on in spirit (John 12:25).

There will be times in our own lives when we may need to humble ourselves before others, perhaps people in positions of great authority. We may do so at a risk to our own lives, for the sake of those who cannot save themselves. In those moments, we too can be as calm, courageous, and faith-filled as Esther—*if* we prepare ourselves as this queen did. *If* we truly believe that when we humble ourselves, pray, seek God's face, and turn from our ungodly ways, He will hear our voices, forgive us, and restore us (2 Chronicles 7:14). And *if* we fix our focus on the Lord of all, placing our ponderings in the hands of the King of Kings. For God has promised that He will keep in perfect peace all who trust in Him, all whose thoughts are fixed on Him (Isaiah 26:3).

This idea resonates deeply in the hearts of we who believe in Christ. For He has told us, "Peace I leave with you; My [perfect] peace I give to you; not as the world gives do I give to you. Do not let your heart be troubled, nor let it be afraid. [Let My perfect peace calm you in every circumstance and give you courage and strength for every challenge]" (John 14:27 AMP).

Daily find your peace by seeking God. Fix your focus on Him. Trust that He holds you safe within His grip, giving you what you need no matter what you face.

> *"My peace I give to you."*
> JOHN 14:27 HCSB

God, help me radiate with Your calm.

The Bliss of Risk

Th' enraptured king gave one impassioned look,
And from its place the golden scepter took
And held it forth. That golden shining form
Was like the rainbow beaming in the storm.
The queen dissolved in bliss, in all her charms,
Sinks overpowered within her husband's arms.

As Esther approached the king, calm and cool, her thoughts fixed on God instead of mired in her present circumstances, Ahasuerus became aware of her presence. And "when he saw Queen Esther standing there in the inner court, he welcomed her and held out the gold scepter to her" (Esther 5:2 NLT).

Whew! What relief Esther must have experienced! She, who had risked her life by coming to the king uninvited, was now not just accepted but received with pleasure. She had kept her misgivings at bay, her thoughts that the king may have grown tired of her. She had shrugged off her what-ifs, maintained her faith, kept her eyes on God, done her duty, followed the Lord's will, and now was reaping the reward!

Although her relief was palpable and wonderful, a desire for the king's acceptance wasn't why Esther had put her life on the line. No. She risked her life so that she would be in a better position to save the lives of others. This was the second step on the unknown path that lay before her. The first had been seeking God and His wisdom, power, courage, strength, and confidence in prayer. She still had a long way to go.

Yet God had proven true to her. She had taken a risk of faith and been rewarded for it, bringing her ever closer to her goal. God had revealed Himself to Esther through prayer and made good on His promise to His people as spoken through the words of the psalmist: "The LORD God is a sun and shield; the LORD bestows grace and favor and honor; no good thing will He withhold from those who walk uprightly" (Psalm 84:11 AMP).

When you look to God for support and strive to do the right thing, know that He will favor you. He will hold out His own scepter of acceptance and encouragement toward you. But He won't stop there. He will bless you because you have looked to Him for strength (Psalm 84:5). And He will make sure you "go from strength to strength [increasing in victorious power]" (Psalm 84:7 AMP).

Today, spend some time with God. Allow Him to fill you with His wisdom and power. Know that every step you take with Him will bring you exactly where He wants you to be: at the right place in His plan.

O LORD of hosts, how blessed and greatly favored is the man who trusts in You [believing in You, relying on You, and committing himself to You with confident hope and expectation].
PSALM 84:12 AMP

What a relief to be walking with You, Lord.
Bless my life as I commit each step to You. Amen.

The Nearness of a Power Unseen

The joy was mutual, and a power unseen
Was near to favor Persia's pious queen.
The king on Esther fixed his eager look,
Embraced his spouse, and thus in kindness spoke. . . .

It's easy to allow misgivings to plague our lives, to keep us from doing what God would have us do. Our worries and fears work together in full force to trip us up, send us on imaginary daydreams, keep us from moving forward, deter us from our path. We work up fictional scenarios on the movie screens of our minds, sure that what we've seen is how things will play out. Front and center is the person who hasn't called us for weeks. Perhaps he doesn't like us anymore. Perhaps he'd be glad to get rid of us, just as he did the girl before. Perhaps he'll use any pretext to replace the one whose charms and beauty he has grown tired of.

Yet Esther had just finished spending three days and nights growing closer to the Lord than perhaps she had ever been before. It was the strength she'd gained in His presence that helped her to do what she had promised—approach her king without an invitation to do so, an act that could mean her death. And as she did so, "a power unseen was near to favor Persia's pious queen."

The king's acceptance of Esther was not only a relief to her but a confirmation that God was near. She had sought His help, relief, and wisdom, calling upon His very presence to be with her, and He hadn't let her down. She had thrown herself upon God and in return had received the "love, pity, and mercy" (Isaiah 55:7 AMPC) He promised.

God understood what Esther had been thinking (1 Chronicles

28:9). When she came seeking Him with her concerns and meandering visions of what might happen, He allowed her to draw close, take on His strength and power, and focus on *His* truth. And He stayed by her side while she stepped forward into His grand plan. She cast down every false thought and kept her eyes on the Lord God so that she could get closer to the knowledge of God's truth in her life (2 Corinthians 10:5).

Perhaps something heavy is pressing upon your own heart. All different kinds of scenarios have played out in your mind, not only confusing you but inhibiting you from moving forward.

Today seek your Lord. Allow Him to search your mind. Be willing to walk His way. And He, that unseen power, will draw near to you, removing every false thought and leading you to victory step by step.

> *Seek GOD while he's here to be found,*
> *pray to him while he's close at hand.*
> ISAIAH 55:6 MSG

Lord, stay near to me and show me
Your truth in each circumstance I face.

Above and Beyond

"Why does Queen Esther anxiously resort
To meet the king within the inner court?
What are the burdens that oppress thy breast?
What thy petitions? What thy great request?
The king will hear and answer all thy prayer;
The queen shall half my royal kingdom share."

I magine being Esther, a former orphan girl who became a queen. She's living in the palace of the grandest kingdom of all when her cousin Mordecai brings her dire news: Because of the decree her husband signed at the evil Haman's suggestion, her people will be wiped off the map within a year's time.

Seeing no other alternative but to plead before the king for the lives of her people, Esther asks Mordecai to have the Jews fast and pray for her for three days. Then she will approach the king without being invited, an action that might very well result in her death. *And* she will do so knowing in the back of her mind that Haman is her husband's current favorite, and she has become a queen somewhat forgotten and perhaps out of favor.

Now here she is, three days later, standing before that same king, feeling the nearness and power of God surrounding her. And, as God would have it, not only is her life spared by her king, but she is welcomed by him. And he doesn't just welcome her—he's concerned about her welfare, anxious for her, wanting to know what caused her to take such a drastic action as to come before him without first being called.

Ahasuerus wants Esther to lay down at his feet whatever burdens she's carrying. He vows to listen to what she has to say and answer her petition, whatever it might be. He says, "Whatever you want, even to half the kingdom, will be given to you" (Esther 5:3 HCSB).

All that Esther requested of God is being given to her—and so much more besides! Not only has she escaped the jaws of death, but because of her husband's longing to do all he can to ease her mind and heart, she is offered half his kingdom!

God has proven to her that those who seek after Him will lack no good thing (Psalm 34:10)! She has trusted in her God and He has not only shielded her from death but helped her (Psalm 115:11–12), doing far beyond what she ever could have asked or imagined (Ephesians 3:20).

Today, whatever your burden, go to God. Let your load slide off your shoulders and land at His feet. Trust Him to give you all good things—including half His kingdom!

God can do anything, you know—far more than you could ever imagine or guess or request in your wildest dreams! He does it not by pushing us around but by working within us, his Spirit deeply and gently within us.
EPHESIANS 3:20 MSG

I praise You, Lord, for doing more than I could ever ask or imagine!

Soul Talk

Fair Esther cleaving to the sovereign's side,
In gentle tones thus modestly replied:
"The king is gracious: let it please my lord
To sit with Haman at my evening board,
And share the pleasures of the genial feast.
The king shall come—Haman the honored guest."

The king spared Esther's life. His concern about the anxiety she must have been experiencing to approach him in such a way had touched his heart, prompting him to welcome her, eager to allow her to unburden herself.

And Esther found the courage to press on. To take her plan even further.

Women like to have a plan. We like to rehearse possible scenarios in our minds and imagine how they might play out. And as we do so, we pray, depending on God's wisdom to guide us. The thing is, we can't make allowances for all contingencies that might arise as our plan unfolds. Sometimes we have to think off the cuff.

Although we're not sure exactly what Esther's plan was, we can assume her standing before the throne wasn't the best of times to beg for the lives of her people. A queen needs a more private place for that type of conversation.

What Esther needed at this point was courage to take the next step forward. That meant asking the king and his favorite nobleman to come sup with her—even suggesting Haman be the guest of honor! This plan bought Esther more time to determine the state of her husband's true feelings for her. And to soften his heart toward her, if needed.

Yet before she requested her husband to come to her banquet with Haman, Esther may have done a little self-talk. She may have needed to encourage herself, because she couldn't be sure what response she would get from her easily influenced husband and king. And she needed to keep her mind clear of doubts and what-ifs.

When we need to encourage ourselves within, when we're winging it, riding on a hope and a prayer, allowing only our faith and determination to lead us into dangerous territory, we might try saying to ourselves, "March on with courage, my soul!"

This wonderful lyric comes from Deborah's song in Judges. God's warriors, led by Deborah and Barak, had just won an important battle. Sisera, the commander of the enemy army, and his nine hundred iron chariots had come sweeping down to attack the Israelites. Divine intervention had brought a sudden storm into the valley, making Sisera's heavy chariots useless. Then the River Kishon "swept [the foe] away, the onrushing torrent, the torrent Kishon" (Judges 5:21 AMPC). Matthew Henry writes, "Deborah's own soul fought against them."*

When you need to shore up your strength, remember God's undefeatable power. Then get your soul in fighting position, telling it:

"March on with courage, my soul!"
JUDGES 5:21 NLT

---

*Remind me of Your divine presence and power, Lord,
and gently shore up my soul when I need courage! Amen.*

*Matthew Henry, *Concise Commentary on the Whole Bible,* https://biblehub.com/commentaries/judges/5-21.htm

Influencers

The king well pleased the favored noble calls,
To feast with Esther in her private halls.
The food, the wine, and female charms, excite
Most joyful feelings on that banquet night.
Fair Esther's blandishments of love had power
To win, and conquer, in that genial hour.

Hearing Esther's request to have him and his prime minister Haman attend her banquet, King Ahasuerus turned to his servants, saying, " 'Hurry, and get Haman so we can do as Esther has requested.' So the king and Haman went to the banquet Esther had prepared" (Esther 5:5 HCSB). What a feast—with delicious food and superb wine, not to mention the company of a beautiful queen—it must have been. And there, not only did the wine flow, but "Fair Esther's blandishments of love had power / To win, and conquer, in that genial hour."

We can make several observations here. The first is that the king's loyalty to his queen was still alive. When Esther made a request, the king commanded Haman to obey, and to hurry to do so.

The second is that God continued to work behind the scenes. He was empowering Esther, who knew the truth of the evil Haman, to entertain her guests, to lavish them with good wine and drink, to play the heartwarming and welcoming hostess to a monster of a man.

The third is that the king's heart was still firmly in God's hands. And He was allowing the power of love—from wife to husband's heart—to make Ahasuerus putty in Esther's hands. If she had lost any favor from her recently absent husband, she easily gained it back.

The fourth is that Haman is loving this attention. His already puffed-up ego must have grown ten times that day. Who else in the kingdom was held in as high esteem as he—to be entertained and enjoy lavish food and drink with both king *and* queen?

The fifth is what was influencing the men in this scene. Haman's actions were the reason for this banquet. It was wounded pride and anger that prompted him to get the king to sign an edict to annihilate the Jews. And the attention he was now receiving from the royals was continuing to massage his unduly inflated ego and satiate his pride.

Ahasuerus, who had been a bit absent as a husband and careless as a king, was being influenced not only by the satisfaction of his typical earthly desires—food and wine—but also by his beautiful wife's attentions.

Both men were influenced by worldly goods and blandishments, things that fed their egos, lusts, pride. Esther alone was influenced by and acting under the direction of the all-powerful God of love.

Many waters cannot quench love, neither can floods drown it.
SONG OF SOLOMON 8:7 AMPC

Lord, may Your love be all that influences me.

A Kingly Offer

"What cares, Queen Esther, fill thy anxious breast?
What thy petition? What thy great request?
The king will hear and answer all thy prayer;
The queen shall half my royal kingdom share."

For the second time (the first being Esther 5:3), the king asked Esther what was bothering her. Any petition she asked, he promised to grant. In fact, he was willing to give her half his kingdom!

Ahasuerus, like many husbands, thought throwing money or gifts or jewelry in his wife's direction would make everything all right! Perhaps some men think that because in certain cases it happens to be true. It's very possible King Ahab's wife Jezebel and her desires were appeased by riches. In fact, 1 Kings 21:25 says, "No one else so completely sold himself to what was evil in the LORD's sight as Ahab did under the influence of his wife Jezebel" (NLT)!

We know the tinkling of coins—1,100 pieces of silver to be exact (Judges 16:5)—was what encouraged Delilah to discover and then betray Samson's secret of strength. And Proverbs tells us a prostitute will bring a man to poverty (Proverbs 6:26)!

Yet Esther could be neither bought nor sold. Nothing the king could offer would deter her from her determination to save her people. No tinkling of coins could turn her head nor steal her heart from her purpose. The only thing she coveted was seeing her people saved from a massacre. She knew her security lay in God and not in earthly treasures.

Have there been times when money has made you deviate from your God-given path? Jesus warns us against hoarding up treasurers here on earth and encourages us to seek first not just the kingdom of God but His way of doing and being (Matthew 6:19, 33). As we follow Him, all we need will be provided in abundance.

When Esther made her decision to decline the king's offer, she found herself on the right path. For she knew that riches were fleeting (Proverbs 23:5) and that true treasure would be laid in the lap of she who was faithful to God (Proverbs 28:20). Esther's faith in God kept her on the right road. And it will be your faith in Jesus that keeps you on yours.

So today and every day, pray for God to give you spiritual wisdom, the kind of insight that will help you grow in your knowledge of Him. Pray "that your hearts will be flooded with light so that you can understand the confident hope he has given to those he called—his holy people who are his rich and glorious inheritance" (Ephesians 1:18 NLT). In so doing, you'll not only keep your feet on God's path but find all the treasure you need therein.

Steep your life in God-reality, God-initiative, God-provisions. . . .
You'll find all your everyday human concerns will be met.
MATTHEW 6:33 MSG

You, Lord, will always be my true treasure.

Reckless Confidence in God

"Most gracious is my lord. The king can roll
The heavy burden from his handmaid's soul.
Be this, O king, the pleasing, hopeful sign.
Again with Haman share my feast of wine.
To morrow I will make my burden known,
And bow a suppliant at the sovereign throne."

Having once more been offered half her husband's kingdom, Esther once more declined. Instead, she told Ahasuerus, "This is my request and deepest wish. If I have found favor with the king, and if it pleases the king to grant my request and do what I ask, please come with Haman tomorrow to the banquet I will prepare for you. Then I will explain what this is all about" (Esther 5:7–8 NLT). And the king acquiesced.

Esther, knowing the Lord's timing was best, didn't rush ahead. Although she didn't know all that God knew, neither the parameters nor the specifics of His strategy, her heart trusted in His plan. Each step of the way, Esther searched her heart, saw God there, and followed His leading. She maintained what one might call a reckless confidence in God.

Some say this was an opportunity that Esther missed. Perhaps even the second opportunity! For the king welcomed her when she first approached the throne—even though she had not been invited! But in those moments when it seems as if an opportunity has been missed, we often see God's hidden power gained.

We may have our own plans in our minds. We have an idea of what we want to accomplish. We have a vision of the end goal. But only when we allow God to direct our steps will we reach that goal.

Imagine being Esther. The lives of your people—men, women, children, babes—are on the line. They are due to be slaughtered in a year's time. And here you are, feasting with your husband, the most powerful man in the kingdom—and his second in command, the evildoer who worked up this scheme to wipe your people off the face of the earth.

What you'd like to see is God strike Haman down with a bolt of lightning. Or have him be trampled to death by horses (2 Kings 9:33) or eaten by bears (2 Kings 2:23–24) or killed by a tent peg driven through his skull (Judges 4:17–21). The last thing you want to do is spend another night wining and dining him.

Yet when Esther searched her heart, God directed her to wait. And her postponement, her deliberate delay to make room for God's will to have its way, allowed God to set the stage, to position the characters of this story in such a way that Esther and her people would have the ultimate victory—no horses, bears, or mallets needed!

A man's mind plans his way, but the Lord
directs his steps and makes them sure.
Proverbs 16:9 ampc

Help me, Lord, to wait on You, knowing You have the best plan.

True Joy

Haman was joyful on that festive day;
Proudly he left the banquet to display
At home his honors, and his friends to greet,
Assembled at his sumptuous, princely seat.

Haman had just been wined and dined by a powerful king and his breathtakingly beautiful queen. And things went so well that he would be doing it again tomorrow night! How much joy can one man hold?

Haman was at the height of happiness. He had power, being second only to the great King Ahasuerus. He'd soon be rid of a tiresome old Jew who needed to learn a hard lesson. And waiting for him at home were his own wonderful wife and sons, not to mention his friends. He, this prince of joy, couldn't wait to tell them all he had experienced and what was on the plate for tomorrow.

We all experience moments of joy when our heads spin with happiness, whether it's due to the arrival of someone we love, an upcoming promotion or raise, the winning of an award or prize, or a good report from the doctor. All these things can raise our spirits. But they are not the source of our joy.

The Bible tells us our true delight, our true joy, is found in God. For "the joy of the LORD is your strength and your stronghold" (Nehemiah 8:10 AMP).

A state of deep gladness and calm comes from knowing God is our all in all. In His Word we find the joy that puts a spring in our step and a song in our heart. When we are down in the mouth, we can turn to Him and He will fill us with good things (Psalm 103:5)—above and beyond what we ever imagined or thought. In His Word we discover overwhelming delight and gratitude in the knowledge that God loved us so much He gave His one and only Son so that we would be forever united with our Father (John 3:16). And nothing can separate us from His love (Romans 8:31–39)—ever.

We can find joy in the Lord, strength in Him who is our stronghold, recognizing He not only forgives us but separates us from our wrongdoings as far as the east is from the west (Psalm 103:12). Our hearts overflow with happiness as we realize He sends His angels to encamp around us (Psalm 34:7), to guard us and lift us up so we won't stumble (Psalm 91:11–12). Because of God in our lives and hearts, we have the joy of experiencing the peace that passes any earthly understanding (Philippians 4:7).

What a blessing to be joyful when God is at the root of our joy!

> *In Your presence is fullness of joy; in Your*
> *right hand there are pleasures forever.*
> PSALM 16:11 NASB

My joy, Lord, is all wrapped up in You! Thank You! Amen.

Wrath Roused

He passed the palace gate, and when he saw
That Mordecai refused the royal law,
His wrath was roused to burning, deadly hate.
And still he curbed his ire, resolved to wait
The coming of the appointed hour, when all
The race of Mordecai in death should fall.

Full of food, wine, and himself, Haman was gleefully tripping along after his banquet with the king and queen of Persia. And who did he run into when he passed the palace gate? Mordecai. The thorn in his evil side. This one who did not, would not bow. The man who refused to obey the law, to pay the wonderful and noble prince the respect he deserved.

The Bible tells us that when Haman "saw Mordecai sitting at the palace gate, not standing up or trembling nervously before him, Haman became furious. However, he restrained himself and went on home" (Esther 5:9–10 NLT). The anticipation of the future demise of the old Jew helped to curb Haman's deadly ire as he resolved to bide his time until not only Mordecai but all those belonging to his race were wiped off the face of the earth.

Neither the things that gave Haman joy nor the things that stole his peace were from God. That was how far Haman was removed from the Holy One's presence.

Yet who are we to judge this man? Are we not, to some degree, ones who also find our peace, joy, and hope in things that are not of God?

Remember the girl who always looked down on you in high school? When you envision seeing her at the ten-year reunion, isn't there some part of you that hopes she isn't as pretty as she used to be? Or perhaps doesn't have as good a job or as many children as you do? Or maybe you have some vengeful feelings for the coworker who was never impressed about your recent pay raise or promotion.

Alexander Whyte writes, "Diabolically wicked as our own hearts often are with jealousy and revenge, at the same time, our hearts are so held down and covered by religion and civilization that we do not know ourselves. There is no difference, says Paul. All vices are in us all, says Seneca; only all vices are not equally extant in us all."*

Granted, Haman's vices were working overtime and hopefully were much greater than our own will ever become. Yet this passage prompts us to look within. To see where we ourselves may be falling short. To consider the thoughts going through our own minds. To be more conscious of our own evil inklings and to take them before the Lord before they lead us down the wrong path, away from the Father (1 John 2:15–17).

> *Throw off your old sinful nature and your former way of life, which is corrupted by lust and deception. Instead, let the Spirit renew your thoughts and attitudes.*
> EPHESIANS 4:22–23 NLT

Renew me, Lord, through and through!

*Alexander Whyte, *Bible Characters from the Old and New Testaments* (Grand Rapids, MI: Kregel Publication, 1990), 420.

The Wicked Haman's Lamp

Arrived at home, the haughty Haman calls
His favored friends within his princely halls;
Speaks of his wealth, his honors, high estate,
And how the princes, nobles, on him wait.
Tells how the king has set his royal throne
O'er all the counselors, and near his own.

When the actions (or inactions) of others tear at the egos of the prideful, they will try to appease their vexation by boasting about themselves or their families, accomplishments, or status. And most likely they will do so in front of people who already know how successful they are. That's just what we find Haman doing.

After his brief encounter with Mordecai, who would not bend his body to him, Haman curbed his anger and headed home. There he regaled his hearers with the fact that he had ten sons (Esther 9:10), was King Ahasuerus's right-hand man, garnered everyone's (well, almost everyone's) unflagging respect, held the top spot in the rank of princes, and had a seat near the king at work (Esther 5:10–11). Perhaps he even imagined himself as Ahasuerus's equal. Maybe he envisioned himself sitting on that throne one day. Whatever his ambitions, Haman was most likely playing the same tune they'd all heard before.

God doesn't like people who are so full of themselves: "Haughty and arrogant eyes and a proud heart, *the lamp of the wicked [their self-centered pride], is sin [in the eyes of God]*" (Proverbs 21:4 AMP, emphasis added). And you can be sure God was keeping His eye on Haman. For He is well acquainted with those of Haman's ilk who act "with overbearing and insolent pride" (Proverbs 21:24 AMP). And so are we.

Although we may feel powerless against rich, powerful, arrogant fools such as Haman, we can find comfort knowing that "the LORD's curse is on the household of the wicked, but He blesses the home of the righteous" (Proverbs 3:33 HCSB), and that "the wise will inherit honor, but He holds up fools to dishonor" (Proverbs 3:35 HCSB).

The last scene between Mordecai and Haman is an excellent picture of the difference between the righteous and the prideful. For we see the unbending Mordecai unafraid before this rich and powerful nobleman. "Mordecai didn't rise or tremble in fear at his presence" (Esther 5:9 HCSB). Mordecai's fortitude must have provoked the prideful Haman even more. For although he exercised some self-control over his anger, we can imagine him at least stomping off as he made his way home.

May we never behave like Haman but rather like the righteous Mordecai, the one God would not only bless but honor.

> *He who trusts confidently in his own heart is*
> *a [dull, thickheaded] fool, but he who walks*
> *in [skillful and godly] wisdom will be rescued.*
> PROVERBS 28:26 AMP

May I always walk in Your wisdom, Lord, not my own. Amen.

Haman's Lost Soul

And Haman said: "Queen Esther too delights
To share with me the genial, festive rites.
I and the king this day were called to join
Her social banquet, and her feast of wine.
To-morrow am I called to grace the board
With happy Esther, and her happier lord."

*a*fter regaling his guests with an account of his wealth, honors, family, employment, and status, Haman added, "And that's not all! Queen Esther invited only me and the king himself to the banquet she prepared for us. And she has invited me to dine with her and the king again tomorrow!" (Esther 5:12 NLT).

The way Haman trusted in and set his heart on status and riches instead of on God may remind us of the warnings found in many stories and proverbs in God's Word (Psalm 62:10; Proverbs 11:28). We can see how he had already forfeited his soul (Mark 8:36), loving money and what it could bring him more than anything else (1 Timothy 6:9–10). We also know it was only a matter of time before the forfeiture of his soul led to the demise of himself, his children, and his estate. Haman's pleasure in his wealth, status, and ease, which would soon turn into his agony, brings to mind one of Jesus' parables.

Once there was a rich man whose land was very productive. He wondered what he might do if he didn't have enough room to store his large harvest. So he came up with an idea. He decided to tear down his current storehouses and build bigger ones! There he would store the massive amount of crops and all his other goods. Then, he thought, he would say to himself, "You have many goods stored up for many years to come; relax, eat, drink, and enjoy yourself!" (Luke 12:19 NASB). But that plan didn't gel with God, who said to him, "You fool! This very night your soul is demanded of you; and as for all that you have prepared, who will own it now?' " (verse 20 NASB). Jesus said, "Such is the one who stores up treasure for himself, and is not rich in relation to God" (verse 21 NASB).

That description fits Haman to a tee. Yet how often do we fall into that same trap? That's not to say we need to be as rich as Haman or this landowner. But chances are we do sometimes trust more in what we can make and put away than in God and His daily bread.

God promises to meet our needs. In Him alone we are to put our trust.

"If you remain in Me and My words remain in you [that is,
if we are vitally united and My message lives in your heart],
ask whatever you wish and it will be done for you."
JOHN 15:7 AMP

Lord, in You alone I trust, for You alone meet my needs.

The Alloy in Haman's Joy

*"But what avail these honors, when I know
That Mordecai to Haman will not bow?"*

So many things had been going Haman's way. First, he'd been promoted to become the king's right-hand man. Then, having experienced Mordecai's disrespect, he'd talked the king into signing and distributing an edict to annihilate not just Mordecai but all Jews in the kingdom. And just that evening, he alone had dined with both the king and his beautiful queen. And was to do the same again tomorrow night!

Yet, when he'd left the palace that night, on his way home, he passed Mordecai, who not only didn't bow but didn't even tremble and shake in fearful respect for Haman! Thus, at the end of his long list of boasts, Haman added, "But this is all worth nothing as long as I see Mordecai the Jew just sitting there at the palace gate" (Esther 5:13 NLT).

Biblical scholar F. B. Meyer writes, "In all earthly joy there is alloy, something which detracts from full gratification; a Mordecai for Haman, because of whom all else availed nothing. The joy that this world gives is at the mercy of unfavorable circumstances, but 'he that drinketh of the water that I shall give him shall never thirst' [John 4:14]."*

There was another rich and powerful man whose joy was stolen. His name was Ahab. And his alloy was Naboth.

Ahab, a very evil king, wanted Naboth's vineyard. After all, it was right next to Ahab's palace. The perfect place for him to put in a vegetable garden. He even promised to give Naboth a better vineyard to replace the one Ahab desired. Or, if that didn't suit,

Ahab would give Naboth the value of the land in silver.

But Naboth refused. Both offers. "So Ahab went home angry and sullen because of Naboth's answer. The king went to bed with his face to the wall and refused to eat!" (1 Kings 21:4 NLT). After finding out what had happened to make her husband pout so, Jezebel (even more evil than Ahab) took matters into her own hands. She had Naboth falsely accused of cursing God and the king. After Naboth was stoned to death as punishment, the vineyard became Ahab's. Problem solved!

What upsets your joy? What turns your smile upside down? What is your alloy, the kryptonite to your earthly joy? To what measures would you go to restore your happiness?

God doesn't want your joy to be based on earthly things. He wants your joy to be deeper than that. He wants you to learn and remember the basics: to teach yourself "to look upon the vexations and trials of life as blessings in disguise."† And to focus your joy, your eternal contentment, on what He provides: Himself.

> *The triumphing of the wicked is short, and the*
> *joy of the godless is only for a moment.*
> JOB 20:5 AMP

> *Continually remind me, Lord, that my*
> *joy is found in You alone. Amen.*

*F. B. Meyer, *Bible Commentary* (Wheaton, IL: Tyndale House Publishers, Inc., 1979), 212.

†H. D. M. Spence-Jones, Pulpit Commentary, https://biblehub.com/commentaries/esther/5-13.htm.

A Grand Plan

Zeresh, of kindred feeling, and who shares
Her husband's honors, and relieves his cares,
And chosen, willing servants, make reply:
"Erect this hour full fifty cubits high
The cross, and ask at morn of majesty,
To hang the Jew upon the gallows tree."

I t's nice to have a loyal spouse. It's even better to have a loyal spouse who doesn't just cater to your moods but leads you down a godly path. But Haman had no such wife.

For after the great (in his own eyes only) Haman explained how Mordecai had stolen his rapturous joy, "his wife Zeresh and all his friends said to him, 'Have a gallows fifty cubits high made, and in the morning ask the king to have Mordecai hanged on it; then go joyfully to the banquet with the king' " (Esther 5:14 AMP).

What was proposed was not actually a gallows where a man might be hanged from the neck until dead. The word "gallows" here is from the Hebrew word for "tree"—meaning both the living tree and the artificial structure to be built. *Barnes' Notes on the Bible* explains, "A gallows, in the ordinary sense, is scarcely intended, since hanging was not a Persian punishment. The intention, no doubt, was to crucify or impale Mordecai; and the pale or cross was to be 75 feet high, to make the punishment more conspicuous."* The idea was that the higher the edifice on which Mordecai was hanged, the more prominent his disgrace, the grander Haman's glory, and the greater the warning to Haman's enemies! And the more paralyzed the courage of the Jews—awaiting an execution of their own—would become.

What a great idea—in their minds. Yet God was at work. And this suggestion fit perfectly into His grand plan.

To get their proposal up and running, Haman's wife, friends, and family suggest he go in to work early the next day and ask the king to allow Mordecai's execution.

It's interesting to note that Haman could have suggested Mordecai's execution long before this. And his king probably would have allowed it, saying, "Whatever. Do as you see fit." But Haman had waited, perhaps even savoring the torture Mordecai would feel when he realized that because of his actions, his fellow Jews were to be wiped out. But because Haman had waited [SPOILER ALERT!], the proposed gallows that were to be built would become the very same gallows upon which Haman himself would be executed.

It was God who stayed Haman's hand from executing Mordecai each time he refused to bow to the nobleman. It was God who brought this idea into the mind of Haman's family and friends. It was God who controlled the situation from beginning to end.

"Courage! Take heart! God is here, right here, on his way to put things right and redress all wrongs. He's on his way! He'll save you!"
Isaiah 35:4 msg

I rest easier, Lord, knowing You are in control.

*Albert Barnes, *Barnes' Notes on the Bible*. Text Courtesy of Internet Sacred Texts Archive, https://biblehub.com/commentaries/esther/5-14.htm

Malice Aforethought

"Then with the king go merrily and join
Queen Esther's banquet, and her feast of wine."

Hearing the plan proposed by his sycophants, to build a gallows on which to hang Mordecai, Haman was "pleased. . .and he ordered the pole set up" (Esther 5:14 NLT). He probably went to bed very happy, dreaming of Mordecai's corpse swaying from a pole built seventy-five feet high.

The rock on which Haman had built his house was about to crumble. Yet, amazingly enough, God had set things up so that Haman had no inkling of what was really happening. He had no idea what Esther's second dinner invitation truly portended. She was not welcoming him to her table a second time to enjoy his company but to reveal his treachery against her people.

Yet Haman was excited about the day to come, most likely looking forward to what would end up being the day of his own death.

One could almost feel sad for this man. For the proud Haman thought earthly riches and gain were the best—and perhaps only—reward in the life of a mortal. And he seemed to find his strength and endurance in malice and hatred rather than in kindness and love.

Yet, as we know, God tends to work in paradoxes. For God, who is love itself, is the most powerful force in heaven and earth. He shows that it is our kindness that lifts us up, not our malice.

One good thing you could say about Haman is that he never pretended not to hate. His true feelings were right out there for people to see. After all, how else would his family have known the suggestion of building a gallows and hanging Mordecai upon it would appease Haman's wounded pride?

There are some who "speak peace with their neighbors, while malice and mischief are in their hearts" (Psalm 28:3 AMP). At least Haman was not that kind of pretender.

The apostle Peter implored believers to "put aside every trace of malice and all deceit and hypocrisy and envy and all slander and hateful speech" (1 Peter 2:1 AMP). For we too were once "foolish, disobedient, deceived, enslaved to various sinful desires and pleasures, spending and wasting our life in malice and envy, hateful, hating one another" (Titus 3:3 AMP)—though perhaps not to the extent Haman was. But once malice finds a way in, it can be like leaven, tainting our sincerity and truth (1 Corinthians 5:8).

Today and every day, make it your goal to be on guard against malice. For you are to "love one another from the heart [always unselfishly seeking the best for one another]" (1 Peter 1:22 AMP).

Make a clean break with all cutting, backbiting, profane talk.
Be gentle with one another, sensitive. Forgive one another as
quickly and thoroughly as God in Christ forgave you.
EPHESIANS 4:31–32 MSG

Help me, Lord, to be a gentle soul to all.

Night Shift

That night the king was restless on his bed.
His heart was wakeful, weary was his head.
Sleep like a shadow flits before his eyes;
The king pursues it, and the shadow flies.
The books of state are read to soothe the king,
And o'er his restless frame soft slumbers bring.

s we enter the sixth chapter of Esther, we witness a change of scenery. We have left Haman to enjoy his happy dreams of revenge and are now at the palace where God is working the night shift. For "that night the king had trouble sleeping, so he ordered an attendant to bring the book of the history of his reign so it could be read to him" (Esther 6:1 NLT).

And here we see that, although God is not named within the story's text, God's providence was in play. About this, Matthew Henry writes:

> *The providence of God rules over the smallest*
> *concerns of men. Not a sparrow falls to the ground*
> *without him. Trace the steps which Providence took*
> *towards the advancement of Mordecai. The king*
> *could not sleep when Providence had a design to*
> *serve, in keeping him awake. We read of no illness*
> *that broke his sleep, but God, whose gift sleep*
> *is, withheld it from him. He who commanded a*
> *hundred and twenty-seven provinces, could not*
> *command one hour's sleep.*

Although the king could not sleep, there were other ways he could have whiled away these restless hours: making love to one of his many concubines, ordering music to be played until he became drowsy, drinking wine or eating some cake. But instead, he commanded that the chronicles of his kingship be read to him.

Perhaps you have had nights when sleep proved elusive. Perhaps it was the troubles of that day and the worries of the one to come that kept you tossing and turning. Perhaps it was a physical malady that prevented you from nodding off to dreamland. Or perhaps it was God doing some night work, acting through any means He could to speak to you, to call your attention to something that might seem trivial to you but would make a huge impact on the life of another.

The next time you find sleep out of reach, make yourself available to God. Ask Him to make His purpose for you clear. Open yourself to receive His prompting, to hear His voice. Then follow His lead. As you do so, you may discover something you neglected to do. A person you had promised to write to or call. A task you had meant to complete ages ago but left undone. Make note of where you were led. Then, after doing what you were prompted to do, take note of the eventual effect that action had on your life or that of another.

I will bless the LORD who has counseled me; indeed,
my heart (mind) instructs me in the night.
PSALM 16:7 AMP

Lead me, Lord, day and night.

*Matthew Henry, *Concise Commentary on the Whole Bible,* https://biblehub.com/commentaries/esther/6-1.htm

Dream State

And Providence directs the recorder's eye
To read the worthy acts of Mordecai,
How he had saved the king, and saved the state,
When men of blood, who kept the palace gate. . . .
And as the reader closed the written roll,
Soft slumbers o'er the royal sleeper stole.

Was it mere chance that the king asked for his chronicles to be read when he could not sleep? And consider what was read to him: "an account of how Mordecai had exposed the plot of Bigthan and Teresh, two of the eunuchs who guarded the door to the king's private quarters. They had plotted to assassinate King Xerxes" (Esther 6:2 NLT).

When all these events are taken together, we can't help but be amazed at the evidence of God's working in not just this situation but every happening in Esther's story! Imagine this powerful king nodding off into dreamland while hearing these words concerning the wise and loyal Mordecai, who because of his actions had saved the life of the sleeper! The poet J. B. Steele puts it into words for us, writing, "And as he slept, the inward waking eye / Still saw the deeds of faithful Mordecai." What an impression must have been laid upon the king's heart and mind when he awoke the next day! What other priorities must have been swept aside to make room for Mordecai!

God may find it easier to vividly impress things upon us when we are in a dream state. He may find our spirits more open to what He would have us know. Whether we're believers or unbelievers, God has a way of nudging our hearts when we are at our most open and vulnerable (see, for example, Genesis 20:1–7).

God once roused the heart of another king of Persia named Cyrus. God used him to fulfill the word He had spoken to Jeremiah the prophet. "The LORD stirred up (put in motion) the spirit of Cyrus king of Persia, so that he sent a proclamation throughout all his kingdom, and also put it in writing" (Ezra 1:1 AMP), permitting God's people to go to Jerusalem and rebuild God's house there!

God also sent a dream to Pilate's wife. During Jesus' trial, she sent a message to her husband, saying, "Leave that innocent man alone. I suffered through a terrible nightmare about him last night" (Matthew 27:19 NLT). She was moved but her husband was not, leaving us with perhaps more questions than answers as to why God may have sent her that dream.

What kind of dreams have you had lately? Consider making a point to tell God, whether you are asleep or awake, "Speak, for Your servant is listening" (1 Samuel 3:10 AMP). And then do what He prompts you to do.

"It came to me in a disturbing vision at night,
when people are in a deep sleep."
JOB 4:13 NLT

Speak by whatever means possible, Lord. I'm listening.

Delayed Reward

The morn has dawned. Ahasuerus calls
His servants round him in his splendid halls.
The king inquires: "What honors have been shown
To Mordecai, who saved the royal throne?"
"Nothing, O king." . . .

The sun came up and the king awoke. God had planted a seed of concern within Ahasuerus's heart, so he asked his servants, " 'What reward or recognition did we ever give Mordecai for this?' . . . His attendants replied, 'Nothing has been done for him' " (Esther 6:3 NLT).

It was not uncommon for kings to express their gratitude for a good deed done by another (2 Samuel 2:6), bestowing a reward befitting whatever service had been performed. But at times the reward was delayed—whether by the king himself or his servants. We don't know whether Mordecai's reward was delayed because his foiling of an assassination attempt against the king had been forgotten or simply because he was a Jew. What we do know is that the discovery of this oversight at this exact point in time—and the king's urgent desire to thank Mordecai—was God's providence.

While serving time in a dungeon, Joseph was put in charge of Pharaoh's cupbearer and baker who'd somehow offended the Egyptian king. When they each had a dream, Joseph was able to explain them. True to his interpretations, the baker was killed and the cupbearer gained his freedom.

Before the cupbearer's release, Joseph asked him to mention him to Pharaoh and help get him out of the dungeon (Genesis 40). But the cupbearer forgot all about Joseph—until, as God would have it, Pharaoh himself had *two* dreams that no one could interpret. Then the cupbearer remembered and suggested Joseph. Upon Joseph's successful interpretation of Pharaoh's dreams, he became Pharaoh's right-hand man (Genesis 41)!

And here again in Esther we have another reward delayed—and later fulfilled at just the right time to save Mordecai's neck!

Perhaps you have performed a service for someone or some institution, and you have yet to be rewarded. Perhaps this lack of acknowledgment has left a sour taste in your mouth, making you reluctant to lift a finger to do another good deed.

But God's Word reminds us that we are to not give up doing what is good. For God promises if we keep doing the right thing, there will be a reward—and we'll get it at just the right time.

So let's not get tired of doing what is good. At just the right time
we will reap a harvest of blessing if we don't give up. Therefore,
whenever we have the opportunity, we should do good to
everyone—especially to those in the family of faith.
GALATIANS 6:9–10 NLT

Help me, Lord, to focus on the good I can
do and not on the expected reward.

Honor or Hanging?

"Who at this early hour
Is in the Court? What man of princely power?"
At early morn revengeful Haman stands
Without the gate, to gain the king's commands,
Upon the gallows fifty cubits high,
To hang that day the faithful Mordecai.

Two men—one a king and one a prime minister—and two radically different intents.

Early in the morning, the king, after a night of little sleep, was eager to bestow a well-deserved but somewhat late-in-coming reward upon a man who saved him from an assassination attempt. But he wasn't sure exactly what that reward should be.

Out of the corner of his eye, Ahasuerus spied someone lurking in the outer court, waiting to be invited into his presence. So he asked his servants who it was. It was Haman, who "had just arrived in the outer court of the palace to ask the king to impale Mordecai on the pole he had prepared" (Esther 6:4 NLT).

Earlier that morning, Haman may have been having trouble keeping his glee in check as he oversaw the building of the gallows on which Mordecai would be killed. For Haman, this murder was a long-awaited desire about to be fulfilled. Now he was watching for the very first opportunity to see the king, to seek permission to carry out this last step in his greatly anticipated revenge upon and humiliation of the Jew who would not bow.

Of course, Haman could have had Mordecai killed at any step along the way. The king could have rewarded Mordecai at any point as well. And here we see the alternate desires colliding on the exact same morning.

Who else but God could have planned it this way? Who else but God—who obviously has a sense of humor—would have these two ungodly men at such utterly cross purposes at the exact same moment of time?

There may be instances when we wonder where God is. Why He allows difficult times to drag out. But we can rest assured that God has everything under control. That not one sparrow falls to the ground without His notice (Matthew 10:29). That everything that happens in our lives is part of His plan. That even nonbelievers have a part to play in saving God's people.

When we are frustrated because of God's seeming inaction, we need to remember who He is: the One who made and set limits on the skies and the seas and set the foundations of the earth (Proverbs 8:27–30), the One who rules over all (Psalm 103:19). And we need to realize that all we need to do is look to Him, knowing all will happen in His good time, including honors and hangings, the rewarding of good and the punishment of evil.

There is a season (a time appointed) for everything and a time for every delight and event or purpose under heaven.
ECCLESIASTES 3:1 AMP

May I put aside my worries, Lord, and remember that You are in charge of all timing. Amen.

Blindside

His servants spoke: "Haman, O king, appears
Without the court, the chief of all the peers."
"Bid Haman enter." Haman, filled with pride,
Stands self-exalted by his sovereign's side.

H aving been announced, Haman, the "chief of all the peers," entered King Ahasuerus's bedchamber (Esther 6:6).

Haman was thrilled because he believed himself to be especially close to the king, needed by His Highness, revered in His Majesty's eyes. Why else would he be invited into Ahasuerus's *bed*chamber? It's easy to see that Haman's exalted thoughts about himself are keeping him from suspecting what God has planned for him.

If Haman had lived in the days of business cards, his would have been embossed with flakes of gold. And his title—whether Chief of All the Peers, Prince of Princes, King's Right-hand Man, or Greatest of All but One—would have been in all capital letters. For his social status meant more to him than all else, including his family, home, salary, and wealth.

There are two types of status: that which is ascribed and that which is achieved. Ascribed statuses are few. The most common are our biological sex, biological relationships, race, religious affiliation, and parents' social class. Our achieved status is somewhat self-explanatory: it's what we have acquired on the basis of our merit. It's a position we have earned or chosen that reflects our skills, abilities, and efforts.

We're not sure of Haman's ascribed statuses. We know he was a Persian man with a wife and ten sons. We know he was not a Jew. And, since he was a prince, we might surmise he was born into the upper social class. What we know of Haman's achieved status is that he was the prince above all princes, the country's prime minister. And he had money to offer in bribe.

Yet all of these things Haman had achieved, all of these things that were ascribed to him, meant nothing in the eyes of God. But because they meant absolutely everything to Haman—who reeked of self-exaltation and pride—he had no idea what God was preparing behind the scenes.

Self-absorption and self-glorification have a way of blinding us. They keep us from seeing the truth of the direction God has given, the way His hand is shifting the scenery, the cues He has given the other actors upon the stage.

Haman, so wise in his own eyes, so full of himself, could not see that God was about to bring him down (Amos 9:2), hard, and bring all his plans to a screeching halt.

> *He who leans on, trusts in, and is confident of his own*
> *mind and heart is a [self-confident] fool, but he who*
> *walks in skillful and godly Wisdom shall be delivered.*
> PROVERBS 28:26 AMPC

Lord, help me trust in You and Your
wisdom far more than my own.

True Wisdom

"What dignity shall crown the man who shares
The king's esteem? What honors shall he wear?"
Vain Haman thought that he, and he alone,
Was best beloved, as nearest to the throne.
And whom, thought he, can Persia's king delight
To honor, save his chosen favorite.

Haman, the blind fool he was, entered the king's most private chamber. And Ahasuerus asked him, "What do you think I should do to honor a man who truly pleases me?"

Haman asked himself—literally "thought in his heart" (KJV)—"Whom would the king wish to honor more than me?" (Esther 6:6 NLT). How self-centered can one guy be?

Have you ever met someone who looks into the pools of your eyes just so he can see a reflection of himself? That's our man Haman. That's why his heart was not a good source for seeking either wisdom or truth.

Yet we all have that challenge in our lives. Because, as God tells us and some of us know from experience, our hearts cannot be trusted. It has been that way since the Fall.

God brought the flood to wipe us out because, unfortunately, He "saw that the wickedness of man was great in the earth, and that every imagination of the thoughts of his heart was only evil *continually*" (Genesis 6:5 KJV, emphasis added). That's not something you'd want to put on a résumé. And it's the word *continually* that really stings.

Things weren't much better by Jeremiah's day. For through that prophet God said, "The heart is more deceitful than anything else, and incurable—who can understand it?" (Jeremiah 17:9 HCSB). Even Jesus joined the chorus, saying, "Out of the heart come evil thoughts and plans, murders, adulteries, sexual immoralities, thefts, false testimonies, slanders (verbal abuse, irreverent speech, blaspheming)" (Matthew 15:19 AMP). None of these are ringing endorsements for checking in with our hearts for guidance.

It's when we trust in God for guidance and wisdom that we'll get blessings from Him (Psalm 24:3–5). Take King David. He was not a perfect human, but he was a man after God's own heart (Acts 13:22). Why? Because he loved and trusted God with the core of his being. And because of this David was a good shepherd for God's people (Psalm 78:72).

Because David's heart was in the right place (in God's hands), he continually asked God for guidance *from* that "right" place, asking Him specific and direct questions (1 Samuel 23:2, 4, 10–11, 12; 30:8; 2 Samuel 2:1; 5:19, 23; 7:18; 21:1; 24:10; 1 Chronicles 13:12; 14:10, 14; 17:16; 21:17)—and getting answers.

When we're looking for solutions, we must seek God, search for Him with our whole heart. And trust Him no matter what. For within God alone lies the true heart of wisdom.

God gives out Wisdom.
PROVERBS 2:6 MSG

Bless my heart with Your wisdom, Lord.

A Fool's Assumption

And Haman said: "The happy man who shares
The king's esteem, and royal honor wears,
Shall have this triumph, worthy of his name,
A lasting honor, and a wide-spread fame."

Here Haman stood, delighting to answer the king's question about what he thought should be done "for the man the king wants to honor" (Esther 6:7 HCSB).

This was something Haman had probably fantasized about his entire life. In his mind, it was only a matter of time before this day arrived. For he assumed that he, Haman himself, was most certainly the man on whom the king wanted to bestow all honor and glory. *Who else could it be?* he asked himself. And his heart, ever willing to please his own ego, answered, *No one but you!*

Matthew Henry writes, "Haman thought the king loved and valued no one but himself, but he was deceived. We should suspect that the esteem which others profess for us, is not so great as it seems to be, that we may not think too well of ourselves, nor trust too much in others."*

Wise words indeed. It's never a good idea to assume how well others think of us. When we do, our words and actions are bound to trip us up.

Maybe you've been in the same sort of situation, hopefully not as ludicrous or painful as Haman's. But chances are you have fantasized moments of grandeur—a prize won, a goal achieved, a recognition of your efforts given. You may have imagined your loved ones around you to see you modestly beam in that moment. The problem arises when you assume that no one is as good as or as well liked as you are to even come close to receiving such magnificent honors.

The remedy for this kind of folly is to refrain from looking for, searching out, or taking for granted the praises of others but rather to strive to please God. That's how the true servant of Christ lives (Galatians 1:10).

For what does it matter if we please human beings, who are so transient (Isaiah 2:22), but disappoint God? Besides, when we please God, even our enemies will not fight with us (Proverbs 16:7)!

Living a life to please God alone takes a lot of pressure off. It reminds us that we need not worry about the new car the Joneses just bought or the number of vacations the Smiths took this year. All we need to do is look to the Lord. Follow the course He has laid before us. And seek honor and congratulations from Him alone.

Why not reevaluate your present life goals? Consider what they may look like in God's eyes. Then use His wisdom to do some refining as you live to please only Him.

> *Whatever you do, do it enthusiastically,*
> *as something done for the Lord and not for men.*
> Colossians 3:23 HCSB

> *Lord, I live for You alone. What would*
> *You have me pursue for You?*

*Matthew Henry, Concise Commentary on the Whole Bible, https://biblehub.com/commentaries/esther/6-7.htm

The Splendor of Stupidity

"The king's most noble prince shall hither bring
The gorgeous garments of the illustrious king.
The royal horse, the scepter, and the crown;
And reverently, humbly bowing down,
On horseback forth shall bring the happy man
Through all the streets and squares of proud Shushan,
Proclaiming: Thus shall dignity be shown
To him whom royalty delights to own."

Haman proceeded to pull out all the stops as he told the king, in elaborate detail, exactly how Ahasuerus should treat the one he wanted to honor. We, the readers, know Haman was not the one to be venerated (as the man himself erroneously supposed) but Mordecai. And as we read of Haman ticking off each item of splendor, we can only laugh at his stupidity, cringe at his craving for recognition, and watch him become further and further entrenched in the trap of humiliation he is unknowingly setting for himself!

Haman told the king:

> *"Have them bring. . .a horse the king himself has*
> *ridden, which has a royal diadem on its head. Put*
> *the garment and the horse under the charge of one*
> *of the king's most noble officials. Have them clothe*
> *the man the king wants to honor; parade him on*
> *the horse through the city square, and proclaim*
> *before him, 'This is what is done for the man the*
> *king wants to honor.'"* (Esther 6:8–9 *HCSB*)

Charles John Ellicott writes in his commentary, "These exceedingly great distinctions Haman suggests, thinking with unaccountable vanity (for nothing is said or implied as to any service rendered by him to the king) that the king must necessarily have been referring to him, and in a moment he is irretrievably committed."*

Here we are reminded of the prayer David prayed to God in Psalm 59. King Saul, jealous of David's popularity among the people and frightened of God's blessing upon him, had sent men to watch David's house, hoping to find him and kill him. But Michal, Saul's daughter, helped David escape through a window (1 Samuel 19). About his enemies, David then prayed to God, asking Him to "let them be trapped in their pride" (Psalm 59:12 ESV). And they were!

Perhaps you have prayed the same prayer, wanting evil people to be trapped in their own lies and wickedness. Consider it done. For whether or not those who plan evil know God, they will be thwarted by Him when they come up against His righteousness.

So no need to worry. Simply count on God, knowing He will take care of every enemy—no matter how wealthy, powerful, or connected—who threatens His plan and people.

*The LORD will not let the righteous go hungry,
but He denies the wicked what they crave.*
PROVERBS 10:3 HCSB

Lord, knowing You'll thwart the schemes of the wicked gives me great comfort. I leave all such people in Your hands. Amen.

*Charles John Ellicott, *Ellicott's Commentary for English Readers.* Text Courtesy of BibleSupport.com. https://biblehub.com/commentaries/esther/6-8.htm

An Unexpected Turn

The king, who held an unresisted sway,
Was firm; e'en Haman dared not disobey.
The horse stands restive at the palace gate;
The humble Jew is clothed in royal state;
The crown is set upon his noble brow;
Officious chamberlains before him bow.

The plot now takes an unexpected turn as we read how Haman had the Persian rug pulled out from underneath his feet. For this was the moment he realized just how far things were careening out of his control.

For King Ahasuerus, still abed, responded to Haman's suggestion by saying: "Excellent! . . . Quick! Take the robes and my horse, and do just as you have said for Mordecai the Jew, who sits at the gate of the palace. Leave out nothing you have suggested!" (Esther 6:10 NLT).

Imagine the shock the king's directive must have sent to Haman's system. He thought his schemes were going well. He thought the king, wanting to glorify him above all others, was going to say, "You, my worthy Haman, are the man I want to honor!" But it was not to be!

At this point Haman began to realize the extent of his folly. That Mordecai—the one Haman had planned, *just two minutes ago*, to ask the king to allow him to execute—was the favored one to receive all these glories he had just enumerated for the king. Mordecai, Haman's sworn enemy. The one whose entire race Haman had plotted to wipe off the face of the earth.

And Haman was, as the king ordered, to hurry, to move quickly to show Mordecai this grand honor. There was no time for Haman to think, to speak, to process this information, this shocking revelation. He had to act under the king's instructions—instructions Haman himself had so enthusiastically recommended for the one the king was to honor—and to do so in haste.

One might wonder if Haman even heard the king specifically describe Mordecai as "the Jew." Or if the king even realized or remembered he'd signed an edict to annihilate all the Jews, at Haman's urging.

But, as we know, Haman had no time to think. He simply had to act, mortified at his error of assumption and now wondering if the rest of his strategy would not only fall apart but result in some grave consequences for his own future.

How wonderfully things had been going—at least in Haman's mind. How ecstatically he had begun this day, believing Mordecai would be hanged.

It's dangerous to "boast about tomorrow, for you do not know what a day may bring" (Proverbs 27:1 ESV). How well Haman knew that now. Or did he?

No one can predict the future.
ECCLESIASTES 10:14 NLT

Lord, help me to leave the future in Your hands
and to focus on what You're doing in my life
in the present. In Jesus' name, amen.

The Pride Fall

And Mordecai on horseback rides abroad,
Preceded by that proud and haughty lord,
Proclaiming: "Thus shall dignity be shown
To him whom royalty delights to own."

What an irony of fate. That Haman himself—until that moment the most important man, prince, and official in the king's court—as commanded by the king, "took the robes and put them on Mordecai, placed him on the king's own horse, and led him through the city square, shouting, 'This is what the king does for someone he wishes to honor!' " (Esther 6:11 NLT).

We can imagine how humiliating this turn of events was for Haman. How much his ego, his perception of himself, must have suffered. What made things worse was the reaction bystanders must have had to this procession. Although the spectators' response to this sight is not included in scripture, J. B. Steele, taking poetic license, writes, "And as the imposing pageantry passed by, / The people hailed the name of Mordecai. / All o'er the land the joyful tidings flew / Of Haman's fall, and triumph of the Jew."

If Haman had just done some research into the God of the Jews, perhaps he would not have devised such schemes against His righteous people. For the scriptures repeatedly tell of God's mighty works on behalf of His people who cry out to Him. God sends plagues to show His power and wonder to the enemy (Exodus 7–10). He parts seas so that His people can cross over on dry land. Once they are safe, He allows the waters to return and drown an enemy army hot on their heels (Exodus 14).

God causes armies attacking the Israelites to become confused and attack each other, leaving His people to pick up the spoils (2 Chronicles 20:1–26). He stops the sun from its courses so His army can win a battle (Joshua 10:12). He even opens up the earth to swallow His own people who have become enemies to His grand plan (Numbers 16:23–33). To those slow in obedience, He either gives an offer they cannot refuse (Acts 9:1–19) or rids the world of them (2 Chronicles 7:13–14). God makes it clear it's either His way or the highway.

Yet the prideful Haman ignored this God to his peril. For this is only the beginning of the end of his story.

Pride blinds us to the plan, power, and very presence of God. For when we depend on ourselves for all things, we find ourselves no longer seeking nor seeing God.

May we acknowledge that "everyone who is arrogant in heart is an abomination to the LORD; be assured, he will not go unpunished" (Proverbs 16:5 ESV) and work to keep any prideful thoughts, emotions, or plans far from our sphere.

> *When pride comes, then comes disgrace,*
> *but with the humble is wisdom.*
> PROVERBS 11:2 ESV

Lord, teach me how to walk humbly with You. Amen.

A Sudden Reversal

To Mordecai these scenes no pleasures bring.
Humbly he seeks his post, and serves his king.
But Haman mourning, and with covered face,
Returned in anguish to his princely place.

*A*fter the impromptu parade showcasing the king's esteem for Mordecai, that still-humble man of God went back to work serving Ahasuerus. But Haman, the man who'd led the horse bearing Mordecai, exited stage left with his face covered, full of anguish and humiliation (Esther 6:12). What a dichotomy these two men present. And how quickly their fortunes were reversed.

Mordecai, a good and humble man, had stayed true to his God, no matter what it cost him regarding his person, reputation, or status. And when his decision not to bow down to Haman brought with it the threat of the destruction of himself and his people, he mourned his people's prospects. He then sent word to his adopted daughter the queen, gaining her aid in righting a terrible wrong. Now, having been honored by the king he continued to serve, Mordecai simply went back to work. There is no word of his ego expanding seven-, ten-, or one hundred–fold. God knows it is safe to bless the humble, for they seek to honor Him alone.

And then there was Haman. As rich and proud as a self-made man could be, he'd maliciously planned his vengeance on those he felt had belittled or wronged him. He'd put out the contract on Mordecai and God's people. But he'd gone too far. And now that the proud man had been brought low, he covered his face.

We have seen the covering of the face before. Jeremiah 14:4 says, "The ground is cracked because there has been no rain on the land; the farmers are distressed, and they have covered their heads [in shame]" (AMP). Even David covered his face in shame, despair, and mourning (2 Samuel 15:30). And we continue to see faces covered in today's news when a now-shamed vile and evil person is arrested. Haman was no exception to this covering of oneself in disgrace.

Proverbs 29:23 reminds us that "a man's pride and sense of self-importance will bring him down, but he who has a humble spirit will obtain honor" (AMP). When we act out of pride, we displease God. He sets up for a big fall those who put their own selves before Him.

Perhaps you yourself have let your pride get ahead of you. And before you knew it, you'd fallen flat on your face. Hopefully that experience got you back on the right path. If not, be assured that the next fall will be even harder. So keep yourself humble. Both you and God will be honored as a result.

> *Pride lands you flat on your face;*
> *humility prepares you for honors.*
> PROVERBS 29:23 MSG

Lord, help me maintain a humble spirit—
in both Your eyes and mine. Amen.

To Home Runs Haman

And [Haman] all dismayed, dejected, and forlorn,
Made known the doings of that dreadful morn.
With equal wonder, and with equal fear,
His consort listens, and his wise men hear.

Shame covering his face (Psalm 44:15 ESV), Haman ran home (Esther 6:12), hoping to find some solace there. Or perhaps hide until he could recover his composure and rebuild his pride. There he, perhaps upset and frightened, unburdened himself.

If you have a tender heart, you might feel a bit sad for Haman. Yes, he is a very proud and evil man. A Hitler of sorts. Yes, he has all things—*but* he has not God and the companionship of fellow believers.

Perhaps you have, during a stressful time, turned to God and your church family for encouragement and direction, compassion and hope. And after leaving their company, refreshed and renewed, strengthened and hopeful, you wondered, *How can anyone survive this life without the light and love of God and fellow believers?*

Remember the first time we encountered Haman at home? He'd just been singled out by Queen Esther for a banquet with herself and her husband the king. He'd left the palace in high spirits. But when he saw "Mordecai in the king's gate, that he neither rose nor trembled before him, he was filled with wrath" (Esther 5:9 ESV). Once home, he told his wife, family, and friends about the wonderful banquet and Mordecai the unbending Jew. Wanting to alleviate Haman's ire, they told him to build a gallows and hang Mordecai upon it. Bad advice any way a believer looks at it but a splendid idea to the proud Haman and his cohorts.

When you ask the advice of worldly people—those who believe in the power of money, conventions, and status—that advice is going to differ substantially from what you would receive from God, His Word, and other believers. And now we see the consequences of the guidance Haman took to heart.

If you have one foot in the world and one in the faith, you might ask for advice from both sides. But it's God, His Word, His Spirit, and fellow believers you should trust. For God and His people are the best support, guidance, and comfort for you this side of heaven. Together we "stir up one another to love and good works" (Hebrews 10:24 ESV); "bear one another's burdens" (Galatians 6:2 ESV); are "mutually encouraged" (Romans 1:12 ESV); and know "God abides in us" (1 John 4:12 ESV).

When you need help, comfort, love, and direction, run to God, His Word, and your church family. There you will receive all you require—and more.

If we walk in the light, as he is in the light,
we have fellowship with one another.
1 JOHN 1:7 ESV

To You, Your Word, and my fellow believers I run.
For You are my light, my love, my all.

Doomed

And spouse, and friends, thro' these dark signs descry
The fall of Haman, and the rise of Mordecai;
And thus they said: "Thy cherished scheme can n'er prevail
Against the seed of God, the race of Israel."

*A*fter Haman told his wife Zeresh, his friends, and the king's wise men all that had happened to him, they said, "If Mordecai, before whom you have begun to fall, is of the Jewish people, you will not overcome him but will surely fall before him' " (Esther 6:13 ESV). Not words Haman had wanted or hoped to hear.

When Haman was brimming with boastful pride, the advice was to hang Mordecai. But now that the tide had turned, he was given no advice. Just a statement of fact: "You're as good as ruined" (Esther 6:13 MSG). They all realized Haman was on an irreversible course and there was nothing anyone could do to stop it. For Mordecai was of the Jews. No possibility of victory for Haman here.

Perhaps that was how Rahab felt when she sided with Joshua's spies, saving their lives and the lives of herself and her family. For she, also a Gentile, had told them, "I know the LORD has given you this land. . . . We are all afraid of you. Everyone in the land is living in terror" (Joshua 2:9 NLT). Her people had already heard of God making a path through the Red Sea, how He'd done away with a couple of kings, killing them and destroying all their people. She said, "No wonder our hearts have melted in fear! No one has the courage to fight after hearing such things. For the LORD your God is the supreme God of the heavens above and the earth below" (Joshua 2:11 NLT).

Knowing that Gentiles had heard stories about the miracles God worked among His people makes you wonder why Haman and his entourage had even attempted to mess with Mordecai and the Jews! Perhaps they had assumed God's power was latent. After all, His people had been scattered all over the Persian Empire in which they lived. Perhaps this Lord of the Jews had lost whatever power He'd once had.

Yet now, hearing of the sudden and stunning turnaround of Mordecai's fortunes, Haman's family and friends finally realized he was in big trouble and that the course he found himself on could not be reversed.

Reading this portion of Esther's story makes it clear Haman would soon fall into the pit he had dug for others (Ecclesiastes 10:8). Like many before and after him, he was going to break beneath the heavy load of his own wickedness (Proverbs 11:5).

Just one more reason to stay on the right side of God.

The righteousness of the blameless will smooth their way and keep it straight, but the wicked will fall by his own wickedness.
PROVERBS 11:5 AMP

---

*Lord, help me to stay on the right path,
the one You have laid before me. Amen.*

Whisked Away!

And as they talked, the servants of the king
Approached the hall with hurried steps, to bring
The minister of state forthwith to join
Queen Esther's banquet, and her feast of wine.

While Haman was in conversation with his entourage, "the king's eunuchs arrived and quickly brought Haman to the banquet which Esther had prepared" (Esther 6:14 NASB). While Haman was fleet of foot in getting to the first banquet, he may have been dragging his feet to the second. After all, how much worse could his day get?

We've already seen Haman hurrying or inducing speed several times in the book of Esther. It didn't take him long to go from getting angry with Mordecai to obtaining permission from the king to create and distribute an edict to annihilate the Jews. After that sprint, he relaxed awhile as he and the king sat down to drink (Esther 3:15).

Then the king had told Haman to "come quickly" (Esther 5:5 NLT) to Esther's banquet. And he must have hurried there, for it was a command from the king.

Then, once again enraged by Mordecai's refusal to bend his knee or his back at the king's gate, that very same night, Haman determined to build a gallows on which to hang Mordecai, then quickly ordered the poles set up and had it built and ready to go the very next morning!

Early that same morning, as Haman waited to ask the king to authorize the killing of Mordecai, Haman was asked what should be done for someone the king wanted to honor. Thinking he must be the one the king had in mind, Haman rushed to answer the king's question. But he soon found out he was not the one to be honored. *Mordecai* was, while Haman was charged with the actual task of honoring him: "Hurry; take the robes and the horse, as you have said, and do so to Mordecai the Jew" (Esther 6:10 ESV).

Soon after that debacle, Haman "hurried to his house, mourning and with his head covered" (Esther 6:12 ESV), hoping to get a sympathetic ear and some wise counsel at home, neither of which he received.

And now here Haman stood, dejected, hopeless, forlorn. All his evil plans coming to naught. And "the eunuchs of the king arrived and rushed Haman to the banquet Esther had prepared" (Esther 6:14 HCSB).

Haman ran to do evil (Proverbs 1:16; Isaiah 59:7; Romans 3:15–17). In his blind conceit, he couldn't see his own wickedness and didn't think God would ever discover his hatred and evil doings. But soon he would fall (Psalm 36:1–4; 12).

When you're in a hurry, do a quick check-in with yourself and God. Make sure your heart and feet are in the right place.

Desire without knowledge is not good, and whoever makes haste with his feet misses his way.
PROVERBS 19:2 ESV

Lord, help me determine if my heart and feet are in the right place.

Prayer and Action

"Most gracious is my lord. The king can roll
The heavy burden from his handmaid's soul.
Oh! spare my life—my mourning people spare!
This my petition: this my anxious prayer. . . ."

Haman was rushed over to join the king for dinner with Queen Esther. As they were drinking their wine, King Ahasuerus, as he had two times before (Esther 5:3, 6), asked his wife to tell him her petition, promising it would be granted. "Whatever you seek, even to half the kingdom, will be done" (7:2 HCSB). For the third time, he pressed his wife for a reply.

Esther had very much awakened her husband's curiosity. For her to seek an audience with him, to come into his presence unbidden at the risk of her own life, had to mean that something of great weight and urgency was pressing upon her mind. Yet twice she had let his question of what troubled her remain unanswered. Now the king was chomping at the bit, keen to have his query answered.

After hearing those encouraging words from her husband, Esther took a deep, calming breath and began her reply. She warmed him up with, "If I have obtained your approval, my king, and if the king is pleased. . ." Here a drumroll would not be amiss. For what follows is just the beginning of Esther's big reveal: "Spare my life—this is my request; and spare my people—this is my desire" (Esther 7:3 HCSB).

The secret was finally out! And we discover what Esther was truly made of.

Here we have a woman with a massive problem. One that was brought to her attention, explained to her, then laid at her door. After discussing the situation with her adoptive father, Mordecai, she commanded that all the Jews in Susa pray, just as she and her maids would pray. Then, even though it was against the law, she would go in to see her husband uninvited. And if she perished, she perished. If not, she would ask King Ahasuerus to help her reverse an irreversible death warrant against her people.

Our bold and determined, yet troubled, Esther didn't just pray to God (4:16) about the gravity of her situation. She didn't just talk about it, spouting off a plan or two and then forgetting about it. She also acted. F. B. Meyer writes, "She took such measures as were possible to gain the king's favor, to awaken his curiosity, and to appeal for his help."

When you find yourself in a dire situation, pray. Then act as God leads. Although you may not know why certain things happen or what exactly God wants you to do, you can rest in the truth that He has a good reason for everything.

God made everything with a place and purpose.
PROVERBS 16:4 MSG

Lord, help me to pray and then act with courage,
even if I don't understand Your plan. Amen.

The Big Reveal: Part 1

"For we are sold. I and my people all
On one appointed day are doomed to fall.
But still the oppressor's gold could n'er replace
The absence of our peaceful, faithful race. . . .
Oh! spare my life—my mourning people spare!
This my petition: this my anxious prayer."

The king had asked Esther two questions: "What is your wish? . . . And what is your request?" (Esther 7:2 ESV). And she answered them in order: "Let my life be granted me for my wish, and my people for my request" (Esther 7:3 ESV). Then she continued: "For my people and I have been sold to those who would kill, slaughter, and annihilate us. If we had merely been sold as slaves, I could remain quiet, for that would be too trivial a matter to warrant disturbing the king" (Esther 7:4 NLT).

The king's head must have been spinning! His very own wife was a Jew! He suddenly understood the urgency of her situation.

If we step back for a moment, we recognize that this scene seems to be playing out at supersonic speed. All the things God had put into place since hearing the cry of His children were now proving their worth, effect, and importance at this second banquet. In the ten verses belonging to this chapter of Esther's book, we see Haman's plan, object, and very life collapse within a matter of moments.

Both Esther and Mordecai had been allowing God to have His way in this situation. Esther waited to speak until she was sure of God's prompting. Mordecai went from publicly sitting in sackcloth and ashes to, as much as he must have abhorred it, allowing himself to be paraded around riding the king's horse and wearing his robes. Each acted out their individual parts knowing that not only their own lives were in jeopardy but also the lives of all God's people. And the clock was ticking.

Back to the scene at hand. The king had had people come to him before, pleading for their lives to be spared. But this was his wife! She who was "sold to those who would kill, slaughter, and annihilate" her and all her people (Esther 7:4 NLT)!

Suddenly a familiar refrain began rolling around in his head. She was reciting the words of the petition, that now glaringly awful edict he had agreed to, ordering "all Jews—young and old, including women and children—[to] be killed, slaughtered, and annihilated on a single day" (Esther 3:13 NLT).

The king had been deceived into authorizing the death of a beautiful queen to whom he'd not just given his heart but offered up to half his kingdom. To have his coffers filled upon her people's massacre was too much for Esther—and now Ahasuerus—to bear.

> *The plans of the godly are just;*
> *the advice of the wicked is treacherous.*
> PROVERBS 12:5 NLT

Help me, Lord, to be cautious about whom I take advice from.

The Big Reveal: Part 2

"Who, who, O queen, can dare this deed to do?"
"The enemy, the oppressor of the Jew,"
The calm, the heaven-supported queen replied,
"Is here; this wicked Haman at thy side."

*N*ow it was the king's turn to ask Queen Esther a few questions. Because of his rage, his questions came out in a spurt of staccato expressions: "Who is he, and where is he, who dares to do such a thing?" (Esther 7:5 AMP).

Why would the king ask such questions? He must have known Haman was the man behind all these horrible deeds. Perhaps he wondered if Haman and others were a part of that plot against him that Mordecai had discovered and then disclosed (Esther 2:21–23). Or maybe Haman had wanted to kill the queen and decided to hide his intentions by murdering all the Jews at once.

The king's three-part question about who was behind all this didn't hang in the air long. Esther quickly replied, "The adversary and enemy is this evil Haman" (Esther 7:6 HCSB).

The king must have been reeling. That his head of state, his right-hand man, the one who sat at the king's side that very moment was behind the threat to the life of his queen!

Joseph Benson writes in his commentary:

> He [King Ahasuerus] wonders that any one should
> be so wicked as to conceive such a thing, or that
> any one should be so bold as to attempt to effect it;
> that is, to circumvent him, and procure a decree,
> whereby not only his revenue should be so much

injured, and so many of his innocent subjects destroyed, but his queen also involved in the same destruction. We sometimes startle at that evil which we ourselves are chargeable with. Ahasuerus is amazed at that wickedness which he himself was guilty of: for he had consented to the bloody edict; so that Esther might have said, Thou art the man!*

What truth we find in these words!

Here we are reminded of Jesus' admonition: "Don't pick on people, jump on their failures, criticize their faults—unless, of course, you want the same treatment. That critical spirit has a way of boomeranging. It's easy to see a smudge on your neighbor's face and be oblivious to the ugly sneer on your own" (Matthew 7:1–3 MSG).

Granted, in Esther's story, there is no mere fault-finding or criticism found in Haman; simply pure evil. But that same inner evil can be applied to the king.

No matter what the degree of sin, judgment, fault-finding, criticism, or evil, it's easy to find more fault in others than in yourself. So make a conscious effort to look within when you see something that disturbs you in others. Then ask God to help you see more clearly.

> *"Wipe that ugly sneer off your own face [so that] you might be fit to offer a washcloth to your neighbor."*
> MATTHEW 7:5 MSG

Help me look within, Lord, before I criticize without.

*Joseph Benson, Benson Commentary on the Old and New Testaments. Text Courtesy of BibleSupport.com. https://biblehub.com/commentaries/esther/7-5.htm

Exposed

The man of blood before that gentle eye
Recoiled, as smitten by the power on high;
While all the memories of the bloody scroll
Arose afresh within the sovereign's soul.
He seeks his garden; there, perplexed, he stands
And wonders at his own unjust commands.

*a*ll had been revealed. Every secret was out, each person's heart laid bare.

Esther had revealed that she was a Jew and that she and her people had been scheduled for slaughter. She had named the viper who had been sheltered at her mate's breast. His name was Haman, the author of her and her people's fate.

As soon as the viper heard her proclamations, he recoiled. It was as if God had looked down from heaven and exposed Haman's darkness with one powerful beam of light.

Memories of the edict that Haman had enticed him to endorse rose up in the king's mind and struck deep at his heart. Now he realized how complicit he had been in Haman's scheme. How much he too was to blame for his wife's life being in jeopardy. And a fresh and intense anger claimed him.

Confused, needing to think things out, Ahasuerus left the food, the wine, the company and headed into his garden.

This seems to be the second truly wise step the king took (the first being his recognition of the good deeds of Mordecai). He was allowing his temper to cool before he made any sweeping decisions. He had removed himself from the immediate situation, taken some time to simmer down.

As he strolled along the garden path, Ahasuerus felt he had been too easily duped. To think he had made this scoundrel his right-hand man! Haman not only had gained the king's blind trust but had made him an accomplice to the impending murder of the queen and her people! What a disgrace—what shame now clothed his realm.

Perhaps you too have been hoodwinked by someone, used to further their own ends. When the truth was revealed, you realized you'd been so easily played, becoming a mere pawn in another's scheme.

Anger, shame, and frustration are the usual reactions in such situations. When those emotions rise within you, ask God to help you get some control over your anger. For as Ecclesiastes warns, "Don't let your spirit rush to be angry, for anger abides in the heart of fools" (7:9 HCSB). Allow yourself some time to cool off. Take a long walk to relieve your angst and clear your head. Then follow up that walk with prayer, asking God for guidance on how to handle the situation. And as you pray and ponder, consider what God is teaching you in this moment. That type of reflection will move you from the darkness of your situation back into God's light.

> *People with integrity walk safely, but those*
> *who follow crooked paths will be exposed.*
> PROVERBS 10:9 NLT

> *Lord, help me to live a life of integrity,*
> *consulting You at every turn. Amen.*

Too Late

Proud Haman, conscience stricken, filled with dread,
Saw judgements gathering o'er his guilty head;
And prayed the queen, with agonizing cry,
To spare his life, though justly doomed to die.

While the king lingered in the garden, contemplating the truths that had just been exposed and attempting to rein in his anger, Esther and Haman remained behind amid half-filled wineglasses and delicacies of food.

Having been faced with the king's fury, Haman "stood terrified" (Esther 7:6 HCSB). Filled with fear over what might happen to him and remorse over the plans he had set in motion, he began pleading with Queen Esther for his life (Esther 7:7).

We have seen this behavior before in Scripture in the story of Judas. He too was sorry he had betrayed Jesus and tried to reverse what he had done, to become humble and repentant. Matthew 27:3–4 (HCSB) says:

> Judas, His betrayer, seeing that He had been
> condemned, was full of remorse and returned the
> 30 pieces of silver to the chief priests and elders. "I
> have sinned by betraying innocent blood," he said.
>   "What's that to us?" they said. "See to it
> yourself!"

Upon hearing those words, Judas "threw the silver into the sanctuary and departed. Then he went and hanged himself" (verse 5 HCSB).

Once we've set plans in motion, whether we've intended them

for good or evil, they are more often than not difficult to reverse. Nor can the effect of them be tempered.

Even Sarah, when she thought it would be a good idea to have Abraham impregnate Hagar and to claim the child as her own, discovered how badly well-intentioned schemes can backfire (Genesis 21:1–21). To this day, there is animosity between the heirs of Hagar's son Ishmael (forefather of the Arab nations) and Sarah's son Isaac (forefather of the Jews).

When Reuben found out his brothers had sold Joseph to some passing traders, he was sick with sorrow. Then the brothers made up a story—*and* fabricated forensic evidence to back it up—about Joseph getting killed by a wild animal. All to back up their misdeed. The brothers' scheme caused their father no end of grief, and he refused any comfort (Genesis 37:18–36).

Perhaps there have been times when you too set a plan in motion only to see it career out of control, harming everyone it touched. To avoid such situations, don't rush to implement any schemes. Instead, do yourself and those you love a favor by submitting all your plans to God before you take any action. Ask Him to lead you forward step by step or to allow your idea to fall by the wayside.

He leads the humble in doing right, teaching them his way.
PSALM 25:9 NLT

Lord, I bring all my ideas, plans, and strategies before You. Tell me what You would have me do or not do, what steps I should take or not take. Lead me to do things for You and in Your way.

Bowing to Irony

The king returned, and at Queen Esther's feet,
Now fallen prostrate on her festive seat,
He saw the suppliant, and in wrath he said:
"Will Haman now pollute Queen Esther's bed?"

Haman's wicked scheme began after his promotion by the king, "making him the most powerful official in the empire" (Esther 3:1 NLT). All the other officials of the king would pay Haman the respect due his name and his position, just as the king commanded. All except for Mordecai the Jew.

Mordecai's refusal to bow, to tremble with fear in Haman's presence, had filled Haman with rage. "He had learned of Mordecai's nationality, so he decided it was not enough to lay hands on Mordecai alone. Instead, he looked for a way to destroy all the Jews" (Esther 3:6 NLT). And he found that way by getting the king to sign an edict to do just that.

Now we see Haman standing up in terror, then "groveling at the couch on which Esther reclined" (Esther 7:8 MSG). How far this once mighty man had fallen! How ironic that he who had schemed to destroy the Jews was now groveling at the feet of their queen! And doing so just as the king came back in from the garden!

Whatever leniency the king may have shown Haman now vanished completely. For the king, witnessing this seemingly lurid scene, accused Haman of assaulting his wife the queen. And of doing so not only in the king's own house but in his very presence! It's this final act that seals the cruel Haman's fate.

About this, Charles Ellicott writes in his commentary:

*The king on his return was evidently full of wrath
against Haman, and though he was for the time
God's instrument in averting Haman's wicked
design, his own base and worthless character is
none the less conspicuous. The attempted massacre
had been authorised with the full knowledge and
consent of the king, who yet ignores utterly his own
share of the responsibility. Great and noble ends
are at times brought about by the instrumentality
of unholy men, blind instruments in a purpose
whose end they understand not.**

God will do whatever He needs to do, use whoever He needs to use, to see His plans come to fruition. He used Peter, the disciple who denied knowing Him three times, to feed and love His sheep. God used Paul, a former persecutor of Christians, to preach His Word.

No matter what a person's faith, skill, past, or passion, God can use anyone to further His purposes. Today, ask Him to use you. Then keep your ears and heart open to His message.

*Samuel did not yet know the LORD because he had
never had a message from the LORD before. . . . And the
LORD came and called as before, "Samuel! Samuel!"
And Samuel replied, "Speak, your servant is listening."*
1 SAMUEL 3:7, 10 NLT

Speak, Lord. I am open to Your calling.

*Charles Ellicott, Ellicott's Commentary for English Readers. Text Courtesy of BibleSupport.com. https://biblehub.com/commentaries/esther/7-8.htm

Observant Servants

And as he spake, the attendant servants place
The well known sign of death on Haman's face,
And said: "The gallows fifty cubits high
We saw this morn prepared for Mordecai.
Behold, in Haman's public court it stands;
We wait to know the king's most just commands."

As soon as the enraged king's words—"Will he even assault the queen right here in the palace, before my very eyes?" (Esther 7:8 NLT)—had left Ahasuerus's mouth, servants in attendance "covered Haman's face, signaling his doom" (verse 8 NLT).

Then Harbona, one of the king's eunuch's, revealed even more of Haman's diabolical nature to Ahasuerus. Having seen the gallows on his way to escorting Haman to the banquet, Harbona said, "Haman has set up a sharpened pole that stands seventy-five feet tall in his own courtyard. He intended to use it to impale Mordecai, the man who saved the king from assassination" (7:9 NLT).

Ahasuerus was perhaps shocked to hear that Haman's treacherous intentions went so far as to hang the man the king had honored that very morning! And Esther's stomach may have turned in horror as she realized how close her adoptive father had come to losing his life.

Once again we cannot help but marvel at the way God had planned everything down to the last detail and the last second. The way each participant in this story—Esther, Mordecai, Ahasuerus, Vashti, Haman, Haman's wife and friends, advisers, and various sometimes nameless servants—had a special role to play in accordance with God's timing and prompting, whether they knew Him or not!

From the good to the evil players, God had His hand in the lives of all—and still does today. That's why we ourselves must obey God's promptings to say or do something, whether or not we understand what He has in mind. For we never know what effect our words and actions will have on the entire scheme of things, how our obedience to God's cues may save one, two, or a million lives.

Knowing God is in control of all can also help alleviate the stress we experience when we witness so much evil in this world. Knowing God has a plan—and that His plan is playing out—lessens the angst of seeing the wicked appear successful while God's people struggle to protect their families from famine, war, catastrophe, and disease.

Every day, ease your mind and heart by being obedient to God, knowing that those who do their part, and who wait for the Lord to do His, will win all in the end.

Don't worry about evil people who prosper or fret about
their wicked schemes. . . . For the wicked will be destroyed,
but those who trust in the LORD will possess the land.

PSALM 37:7, 9 NLT

Lord, in You alone I rest and trust as I play
my part in accordance with Your promptings.

Poetic Justice

The sovereign spake: "Be this my fixed decree;
Hang Haman, wicked Haman, on that gallows tree."
The judgement given, the ministers of state
Who guard the law, and on the sovereign wait,
Haman suspend full fifty cubits high
Upon the tree prepared for Mordecai.

The eunuch Harbona had just told the king that the gallows—a sharpened pole that stood seventy-five feet high—Haman had prepared for Mordecai was in Haman's own courtyard. The apoplectic king's response to this new information was, "Then impale Haman on it!" (Esther 7:9 NLT). The chapter ends with the words, "So they impaled Haman on the pole he had set up for Mordecai, and the king's anger subsided" (verse 10 NLT).

Talk about poetic justice! The white-hot rage Haman had felt toward Mordecai, the fury that had prompted him to build the gallows upon which to kill the Jew, as well as the public display he'd intended to make of the event, were now aimed toward Haman himself. Also ironic is the fact that the suggestion to build the towering gallows had come from Haman's own loved ones!

Haman had, in a way, devised the instrument of his own demise. He'd dug a pit for Mordecai but proceeded to fall into the hole himself (Psalm 7:15). In this account we witness how "the godly are rescued from trouble, and it falls on the wicked instead" (Proverbs 11:8 NLT).

All these plans Haman concocted were to end the life of one Jewish man named Mordecai, the one part of Haman's life over which he had no power. Scholars believe that at the core of both fear and anger is the feeling of loss of control. Because Mordecai would not bow to Haman, a fear rose up inside of Haman. For Mordecai not only defied the king's law but was not even concerned that he did so!

Thus, the only way Haman could try to get the upper hand in the situation was to create a plan to destroy not only Mordecai but all those who might share his courage and conviction to bow to no one but their own God! Haman's fear and anger had motivated him to go above and beyond what was necessary to rid him of this thorn in his side. And his entire plan, thanks to God's spiritual law of sowing and reaping, ended up bringing about what he perhaps feared the most: his enemy's salvation and his own execution.

The next time you find yourself afraid or angry, go to God. Ask Him to help you sort out your emotions and give you wisdom for how to manage both. If you do so, you yourself may avoid poetic justice.

The nightmares of the wicked come true;
what the good people desire, they get.
PROVERBS 10:24 MSG

Lord, help me be more aware of my emotions
and use Your wisdom in handling them.

Eternal Justice

The voice of mourning, and the voice of prayer,
Has reached anew Jehovah's gracious ear;
And God exalted moves in majesty
Again to set his chosen people free.
Eternal justice magnifies the laws,
And Heaven protects his people's righteous cause.

Haman's demise, his falling into the pit that he himself had dug, was poetic justice. Another kind of justice is God's eternal justice.

Some people, like Haman, curry the favor of rulers to make their way through the world, to obtain what they desire, to get what they deem justice. But you, as one of God's people, can be sure that you will receive justice from the Lord (Proverbs 29:26), just as Mordecai, Esther, and the rest of the Jews of Persia did.

Earlier in the book of Esther, after Haman had sent his evil edict abroad, the voices of God's people had prompted Him to move. And He did. Perhaps not as quickly as some of the participants in Esther's story would have liked, but at just the right time—*His* time.

God's Word tells us, again and again, that "if we ask anything according to his will he hears us. And if we know that he hears us in whatever we ask, we know that we have the requests that we have asked of him" (1 John 5:14–15 ESV).

Such is the effect and power of the fervent prayers of God's people! Their voices prompt God to move and He does!

And because God's people look to Him for justice, those who are evil become trapped "in the very snares they set, their feet all tangled in the net they spread. They have no excuse; the way God works is well-known. The shrewd machinery made by the wicked has maimed their own hands" (Psalm 9:16 MSG).

Perhaps you're not sure God hears your prayers. His Word tells you otherwise. Before you even call upon Him, He's answering you. While you're still giving Him the whys and wherefores about what you need, He's going ahead and answering your requests (Isaiah 65:24).

Just when Daniel began his prayer to God, while he was still telling God everything he needed to get out, the answer to his prayer was already on its way back to him, delivered by the angel Gabriel (Daniel 9:20–23).

When you see injustices in your own life, don't let fear or worry or anger or angst keep you from praying to the One who can turn things around, the One who will give you eternal justice. Cast your burden on God (Psalm 55:22), knowing He will not only listen to your prayer (Psalm 66:19) but take care of everything (Psalm 50:15).

> *I'm not giving up. I'm sticking around to see what GOD*
> *will do. I'm waiting for God to make things right.*
> *I'm counting on God to listen to me.*
> MICAH 7:7 MSG

To You I pray, Lord. To You I unburden my soul, knowing
in my spirit that You will hear and respond. Amen.

Wealth and Posterity

On that triumphant day the king bestows
On Esther Haman's wealth and princely house.
And Mordecai, by Esther's order, holds
The vast estate, and all the house controls.
On that auspicious day the queen made known
How Mordecai received her as his own.

Haman had been executed. The threat he posed to Mordecai was over. His estate had reverted back to the crown. Then, perhaps to make amends for all the grief he had caused his wife and her people, King Ahasuerus "gave to Queen Esther the house of Haman, the enemy of the Jews" (Esther 8:1 ESV). Any legacy—material or otherwise—Haman had thought he would leave behind had been corrupted into the solitary designation "Haman, the enemy of the Jews." Throughout history he would be remembered as nothing more than one of the most hated adversaries of God's people.

And now, Esther finally revealed her last secret: that Mordecai was her adoptive father. Upon hearing this news (and needing to fill Haman's former post), Ahasuerus gave Mordecai his signet ring, making the Jew whom Haman had hated the king's new right-hand man; Esther, in turn, put Mordecai in charge of Haman's estate (Esther 8:2).

How Haman must have been rolling over in his grave as his family was kicked out of their home, which was put into the custody of his hated enemy Mordecai—the same man now holding Haman's former position!

This is what happens to those who "frantically rush around in vain, gathering possessions without knowing who will get them"

(Psalm 39:6 HCSB). Those who, like Haman, make devious deals, hoping to build themselves wealth, a legacy, a name, a status that, once they become dust, means nothing. Everything they attain might go to a stranger, or worse, an enemy.

None of us know what will happen to the money and possessions we leave behind. We might ask ourselves the same question the author of Ecclesiastes posed: "I must leave to others everything I have earned. And who can tell whether my successors will be wise or foolish? Yet they will control everything I have gained by my skill and hard work under the sun" (2:18–19 NLT).

Hopefully we won't fall into the trap of Haman and others who live to work, to accumulate more and more and more, so much more that they need to rent bigger storage units to hold all they own or buy larger estates to house it all! May we be wise and take another avenue open to us, the one recommended by Jesus, who tells us not to hoard earthly treasure that can easily disappear but to "stockpile treasure in heaven, where it's safe" from corruption (Matthew 6:20 MSG).

Turn my eyes away from vanity [all those worldly,
meaningless things that distract—let Your priorities be mine],
and restore me [with renewed energy] in Your ways.
PSALM 119:37 AMP

Lord, may I focus not on wealth or posterity but only on
heavenly treasures by making Your priorities my own.

The Story Is Not Over

The Jews' great adversary now is dead.
No sword shall cleave the guarded Esther's head.
The faithful man who guides th' affairs of state
Has all a kinsman's heart for Judah's fate.
But oh! the bloody scroll o'er all the land,
From Ethiopia to the Indian stand,
Is calling bitter enemies to rise
And offer up in one great sacrifice.

Although Haman was now dead and Mordecai safe, the danger to the Jewish populace continued because the king's edict still stood. And once again, the queen had to go before the king, risking her neck to save the lives of others. Maclaren's *Expositions* explains:

> *The danger was not past, though she was queen*
> *and beloved; for a despot's love is a shifting*
> *sand-bank, which may yield anchorage to-day, and*
> *to-morrow may be washed away. So she counted*
> *not her life dear unto herself when, for the second*
> *time. . .she ventured, uninvited, into the king's*
> *presence. The womanly courage that risks life for*
> *love's sake is nobler than the soldier's that feels the*
> *lust of battle maddening him.**

Following her heart and taking courage in hand, Esther fell down at her sovereign's feet, weeping, and begged Ahasuerus to do the undoable: "to avert the evil plot of Haman the Agagite and his plan which he had devised against the Jews [because the decree to annihilate the Jews was still in effect]" (Esther 8:3 AMP).

What courage! In this action, Esther expressed and embodied the type of love that Jesus described in John 15:12–13 (and later demonstrated to His followers), saying, "This is My commandment, that you love and unselfishly seek the best for one another, just as I have loved you. No one has greater love [nor stronger commitment] than to lay down his own life for his friends" (AMP). What a friend the Jews have in this queen willing to sacrifice her own life—twice—for her people!

Yet Esther also represents something else this world desperately needs: interceders. In this, she follows the paths of mortal men. Abraham, having learned of the imminent destruction of Sodom and Gomorrah, successfully interceded on behalf of his nephew Lot (Genesis 18:16–33). Moses pleaded with God not to destroy His people over their idolization of a golden calf (Exodus 32:11–14), and He relented. Elijah, wanting the people to know the Lord alone is God, asked Him to reveal His power to His people, which He did (1 Kings 18:1–39). Prompted by the suffering of God's people, Daniel prayed and an angel brought the response (Daniel 10:12).

Because women have sensitive hearts and express fierce love, they too can be powerful intercessors for God. May the Lord draw you to become one of them. For the story is not yet over.

> *The first thing I want you to do is pray. Pray every way you know how, for everyone you know.*
> 1 TIMOTHY 2:1 MSG

> *Lord, give me the courage and passion to pray for everyone I know, every way I know.*

*Alexander Maclaren, Expositions of Holy Scripture. Text Courtesy of BibleSupport.com. https://biblehub.com/commentaries/esther/8-3.htm

Pleading the Cause

Again, uncalled, unguarded, and alone,
Queen Esther falls before the royal throne,
All bathed with flowing tears, all desolate,
A willing sacrifice for Judah's fate.
The extended scepter saved her from the laws,
And Esther rose to plead her people's cause.

The king graciously extended his golden scepter to Esther, saving her neck and giving her leave to address him once again. And she did so with courage, tact, and eloquence.

Esther used her usual approach in addressing the king. As she did in both Esther 5:8 and 7:3, she began, "If it please the king, and if I have found favor in his sight." Then she added two more items to her list of ifs: "if the thing seems right before the king, and I am pleasing in his eyes" (8:5 ESV). In saying "if the thing seems right before the king," Esther was addressing Ahasuerus's ego, making sure he understood that she was submitting to what *he* thought was the right thing to do in this situation. By adding if "I am pleasing in his eyes," she roused the king's ardor, drawing his attention to her inner and outer beauty.

Following these "if" clauses was Esther's request: "Let there be a decree that reverses the orders of Haman son of Hammedatha the Agagite, who ordered that Jews throughout all the king's provinces should be destroyed" (8:5 NLT). Never once did she blame her husband for his part in this murderous decree. She laid all the fault at the feet of Haman. She intimated that since the order was Haman's, the king could reverse it without losing face.

Esther ended her request by baring her heart in an attempt to reach the king's own: "For how can I bear to see the calamity that is coming to my people? Or how can I bear to see the destruction of my kindred?" (Esther 8:6 ESV). Here she appealed to whatever love her king held in his heart for her, hoping he would yearn to remove her sorrow. Who would not be moved by such a request from such a woman?

Esther bravely and wisely used all the tools in her kit, ones she knew would move her husband to action on her behalf or on behalf of her people. And it worked.

Consider how you too can bravely use the tools and weapons you have to move the hearts and minds of others to do good. And to do so with gentleness and humility, using your inner strength, beauty, and courage to inspire others to be the best they can. To plead for the oppressed, to stand up for the voiceless, to make the causes of others your own. To move mountains, however high.

Gentleness, and self-control. There is no law against these things!
GALATIANS 5:23 NLT

Use me, Lord, in whatever way You see fit,
to plead for others. In Your name, amen.

The Despot's Indolence

The prayer was hard to grant. The stern decree,
In name and seal of royal majesty,
Unchangeable remains: and still the cry
Of Esther, and his faithful Mordecai,
Has overcoming power, and to their hands
The gracious king commits his new commands.

*a*fter hearing his beautiful wife's impassioned plea, the king responded, reminding Esther how he had already given her the recently hanged Haman's house—all "because he tried to lay his hand on the Jews" (Esther 8:7 NKJV). We can almost imagine him making this statement while attempting to stifle a royal yawn, as if the king was now bored with the entire affair.

Ahasuerus then said, "You yourselves [meaning Esther and Mordecai] write a decree concerning the Jews, as you please, in the king's name, and seal it with the king's signet ring; for whatever is written in the king's name and sealed with the king's signet ring no one can revoke" (8:8 NKJV).

Just as lazily as Ahasuerus gave Haman his power and edict against the Jews, he now handed the whole matter over to his wife and Mordecai, leaving them to sort out all the details. Not one jot of the new decree required would be written, added, or amended by King Ahasuerus. For he no longer deigned to be bothered with the edicts, the issues, the cruel affair. He, like Pilate, washed his hands of the matter and wanted no more to do with the conflict he had helped to promulgate, the one that would turn his people against the Jews who had served him loyally.

God help us if we ever become like this ruler, allowing ourselves to be corrupted by power and worldly possessions to the point where we find ourselves blind to the needs of others and content to live for and love ourselves alone. Heaven help us if we make our own wills, our own lusts and passions, our guides.

There is much danger in allowing ourselves to be ruled by our lower nature. May we not abandon our godly duties to others by continually aggrandizing ourselves, making ourselves richer while others became poorer in body, mind, and spirit. For in doing so, we will ruin not only ourselves but those around us.

We all reign in our own queendoms. We all have some power and influence, even if it is only over ourselves. And as such rulers, we must put the needs and wants, the cries and pains of others above our own. We must think more of our duty to God's people than our daily delights.

Be content with obscurity, like Christ. And that means
killing off everything connected with that way of death. . .
doing whatever you feel like whenever you feel like it,
and grabbing whatever attracts your fancy. That's a life
shaped by things and feelings instead of by God.
COLOSSIANS 3:4–6 MSG

Lord, may You alone shape my life.

Hope after All

"Be this the order from the sovereign throne,
Which all the provinces shall hear and own."

Two months had passed since Haman's edict in which the Persians were commanded to take up arms against the Jews and destroy them down to the last babe. And for those two months, the Jews must have trembled in terror, wondering where God was in their lives. How could this be happening? Far away from their fellow believers in Jerusalem, they must have felt like sitting ducks, unguarded, alone, forgotten, and forsaken.

Yet miracle of miracles, Haman was executed, the queen had made known her heritage, and a fellow Jew was made the king's right-hand man. Perhaps there was hope after all! Perhaps God did see them and was going to rescue them despite their misdeeds, forgotten loyalties to their homeland, and times of disobedience.

God's people had been in such dire straits before. In Egypt, they suffered under the hands of their cruel masters. When Moses came back home, he and Aaron, on orders from God, asked Pharaoh to let His people go so they could worship Him in the wilderness. Pharaoh not only refused their request but commanded the Egyptian slave drivers to make the Israelites' lives even harder (Exodus 5:1–18)! In response, the Israelite foremen said to Moses and Aaron, "May God see what you've done and judge you—you've made us stink before Pharaoh and his servants! You've put a weapon in his hand that's going to kill us!" (Exodus 5:21 MSG).

Moses then turned to God, saying, "O Lord, why have you done evil to this people? Why did you ever send me? For since I came to Pharaoh to speak in your name, he has done evil to this people, and you have not delivered your people at all" (Exodus 5:22–23 ESV).

Then God reminded Moses who He was, the promises He had made to His people, and the promises He would keep. He, the Deliverer, would save His Israelites.

Later, in the time of judges in Israel, God continued to hear His people cry and continued to deliver them through various men and women, raising up heroes to free His children from their misery. Later He worked through faithful kings and prophets to help His people. Finally, He brought the one and only Person who can deliver all people everywhere, His Son, Jesus the Christ, the Savior of the world.

Perhaps you have felt abandoned and alone. Maybe there are days and nights, months and seasons, when you wonder where God is. Times when you ask Him, "Where are You? How could this be happening?"

Take heart. Remember who God is: the One surrounding you, the One who will save you.

> *"IN HIS NAME THE GENTILES (all the nations of the world) WILL HOPE [with confidence]."*
> MATTHEW 12:21 AMP

Never let me forget, Lord, that no matter how bad things seem, in You I find hope after all.

Faithful in Action

The scribes are called. And now from proud Shushan
To all the provinces the statute ran. . .
Proclaiming every where: "The Jews shall stand."

Having better things to do than write a new edict to protect the Jews, King Ahasuerus gave Esther and Mordecai carte blanche to write whatever decree they desired. In this, Esther and Mordecai resemble a type of Joseph. They had won a foreign ruler's influence; were second in command only to that ruler (Genesis 41:39–43); had come to prominence after defeating a myriad of evils; and used their newly found power to save God's people (50:20).

Yet the similarities don't begin there. For if we go back to the start of both stories, we find that Joseph and Esther each suffered a trauma at an early age: Joseph was sold into slavery by his brothers (Genesis 37:12–36), and Esther lost her parents (Esther 2:7). The physical attractiveness of both Joseph (Genesis 39:6) and Esther (Esther 2:7) propelled them through their stories. Both Joseph's and Mordecai's good deeds were temporarily forgotten but remembered at crucial moments: Joseph's interpretation of the wine steward's dream (Genesis 40–41) and Mordecai's saving the king from assassination (Esther 2, 6). Both stories take a remarkable turn after their true identities are revealed: Joseph to his brothers (Genesis 45:1–15) and Esther to Haman and Ahasuerus (Esther 7:3–4).

Lastly, God's providence is seen working not through miracles but through the chronicled characters to bring about salvation for His people. Just as Joseph told his brothers, "So it was God who sent me here, not you! And he is the one who made me an adviser to Pharaoh—the manager of his entire palace and the governor of all

Egypt" (Genesis 45:8 NLT), Mordecai told Esther, "If you keep quiet at a time like this, deliverance and relief for the Jews will arise from some other place, but you and your relatives will die. Who knows if perhaps you were made queen for just such a time as this?" (Esther 4:14 NLT).

What can we learn from this? That we too can be faithful in action. We too can rise above traumatic beginnings. We too can do good deeds, ones that may be temporarily forgotten but later remembered in crucial moments. We too may have secrets that one day may be revealed, bringing good out of evil. We too may find the courage to be used by God as we selflessly put others before ourselves for the salvation of all.

God wants the combination of his steady, constant calling
and warm, personal counsel in Scripture to come to
characterize us, keeping us alert for whatever he will do next.
ROMANS 15:5 MSG

Teach me, Lord, how to be faithful in action. To rise above
my personal history, to put others before myself, to bring good
out of evil, to find Your courage within me, and to allow myself
to be used by You to change the course of events.

Defended and Delivered

"The Jews shall gather on the appointed day,
Prepared with sword and spear, in dread array;
And cause to perish all their foes who bring
Their arms against the subjects of the king."

The king told Esther and Mordecai that none of his royal edicts could be reversed or recalled. At the same time, he permitted them to do what they could to save their fellow Jews from Haman's evil edict.

On June 25, Mordecai came up with a plan and dictated a new decree, which was taken down word for word by the king's scribes.

This latest edict "gave the Jews in every city authority to unite to defend their lives. They were allowed to kill, slaughter, and annihilate anyone. . .who might attack them or their children and wives, and to take the property of their enemies. The day chosen for this event throughout all the provinces of King Xerxes was March 7 of the next year" (Esther 8:11–12 NLT).

Mordecai's hope was twofold: to ease some of the tremendous distress the Jews were inevitably feeling ever since Haman's edict had been sent out and to give them enough time to prepare for their own defense (about nine months).

Here we can see God taking a stand with His people, just as He promised in centuries past. In Exodus 23 God had sent an angel before His people, to guard them and keep them (verse 20). He told them to listen to His voice, to heed all the angel said (verse 21). God promised, "If you are careful to obey him, following all my instructions, then I will be an enemy to your enemies, and I will oppose those who oppose you" (verse 22 NLT). And by "oppose," God meant He would "destroy them completely" (verse 23 NLT).

Think back to when the Jebusites told King David, " 'You will not come in here, but the blind and the lame will ward you off'—thinking, 'David cannot come in here.' *Nevertheless*, David took the stronghold of Zion, that is, the city of David" (2 Samuel 5:7 ESV, emphasis added). No matter how dire our straits or how bad things may look, we can always count on God to be in our corner. For He is our "nevertheless."

Haman had sent out an edict to annihilate God's people. *Nevertheless*, Esther and Mordecai worked together to ensure that the Jews would be able to defend themselves. For their enemies were God's enemies.

The same is true for us as followers of Christ today. Whoever is born of God is protected by God (1 John 5:18). We may feel trapped, unprotected, and alone. Nevertheless, Jesus is with us (Matthew 28:20). And He will deliver us in our time of need. Even more, He already has delivered us (2 Corinthians 1:10)!

> *If God is for us, who can be [successful] against us?*
> ROMANS 8:31 AMP

> *Thank You, Lord, for being my Defender,*
> *my Deliverer, and my Nevertheless!*

Express Delivery

And now from proud Shushan
To all the provinces the statute ran:
To nobles, captains, ministers of state;
To soldiers, governors, to small and great.

The new decree went out with all speed but differed from the one Haman had sent out.

For this decree was not just delivered "to the king's highest officers, the governors of the respective provinces, and the nobles of each province in their own scripts and languages" (Esther 3:12 NLT) as Haman's was. Mordecai's was sent '*to the Jews* and to the highest officers, the governors, and the nobles of all the 127 provinces. . . . The decree was written in the scripts and languages of all the peoples of the empire, *including that of the Jews*" (Esther 8:9 NLT, emphasis added). Thus, not only did the Jews get their own notice of the new decree, but it was written in their language. They could readily understand that they could defend themselves. This proclamation didn't arrive by word of mouth, as did the last edict. It was written with them in mind!

God had clearly provided His people with an avenue of escape from their grave predicament. He had made sure they understood this unexpected deliverance *and* that it could not be reversed. For though it was written by one of God's agents and endorsed by a pagan king, God Himself was the One providing this recourse. And what He says always stands.

Just as God wanted His people to receive, understand, and act on the edict that would help to save them, He wants you to get the messages He has placed within scripture:

- "Even if it was written in Scripture long ago, you can be sure it's written for *us*" (Romans 15:4 MSG).

- "These things happened to them as an example, but they were written down for our instruction" (1 Corinthians 10:11 ESV).

Are you getting God's message? Are your ears open, your mouth closed? Are you reading and praying? Are you keeping your eyes on the right prize?

Many people have gone before us, paved a way. They have made mistakes we can learn from. And they want us to keep living the life of faith, to get rid of all that distracts us and to look to Jesus, the author of our faith and story (Hebrews 12:1–2).

Whenever you begin to falter, to lose heart, to feel as if the battle is over and you've lost, look at what others endured, how they found their strength, and what God did for them. Read a Bible translation that makes His message clear so that you too can learn to live and love eternally.

God isn't late with his promise as some measure lateness.
He is restraining himself on account of you, holding back
the End because he doesn't want anyone lost. He's giving
everyone space and time to change.

2 PETER 3:9 MSG

Lord, help me to stay in, think on, and live
by Your Word. Help me to get Your message.

A Wondrous Wardrobe

Arrayed in royal dress of white and blue
And purple robes, and golden crown, the Jew,
The chancellor of state, appears with grace,
The joy and honor of his native place.

Unlike Haman, who sat down and drank some wine with the king after his evil edict had been written and delivered (Esther 3:15), Mordecai went out from the king's presence (8:15) with the same grace with which he had entered it. And unlike the confusion the people of Susa had felt at the earlier edict *against* the Jews (3:15), the populace celebrated the new one that allowed the Jews to defend themselves (8:15).

Whereas Haman was full of and served only himself, Mordecai was full of God and served Him and His people. Whereas Haman fouled the atmosphere of the king's court, Mordecai's presence blessed it. Whereas Haman ran quickly to do evil, Mordecai stood to reverse it. Whereas Haman brimmed with anger, Mordecai overflowed with goodness.

All the worldly trappings that marked the corruption of Haman meant naught to Mordecai. He who once dressed in sackcloth and sat in ashes in the public square thought little of the wardrobe that came with his new position. He lived and worked to do the right thing, to help his people, and to serve his God.

Would that today's politicians would fit the frame and develop the spirit of Mordecai rather than that of Haman. For that matter, we all should be as the humble Mordecai, not caring whether we are noticed when we sit in a position below others, nor trembling when we draw the ire of another more powerful than we, nor feeling embarrassed if we don't have a wardrobe grander than others'.

As believers in Christ, we are not to be concerned with our earthly attire but rather, as God's chosen people, to clothe ourselves "with tenderhearted mercy, kindness, humility, gentleness, and patience. Make allowance for each other's faults, and forgive anyone who offends you. Remember, the Lord forgave you, so you must forgive others" (Colossians 3:12–13 NLT). What a wonderful wardrobe that would be!

It's easy to look at others, notice their faults, and determine ourselves to be better than they are. It's much harder to look within. To consider where our callousness may be harming others. Where we are cruel instead of kind. Where we are proud instead of humble, hard instead of gentle, and rash instead of patient. When we spend more time looking at ourselves, we will find ourselves less critical and more forgiving of others.

Today, spend some time looking deep within. Consider areas where you could be doing better. Don't become supercritical of yourself. Just gently seek God's guidance as to how to become a kinder, more loving and accepting you.

Above all, clothe yourselves with love,
which binds us all together in perfect harmony.
COLOSSIANS 3:14 NLT

Help me, Lord, to dress myself in
love today and every day. Amen.

Decree Received with Joy

The Jews receive with joy the new decree,
And all their souls o'erflow with ecstasy.

The decree Mordecai had dictated had been sent to all corners of the Persian Empire. And "the same decree was proclaimed in the fortress of Susa" (Esther 8:14 NLT). "And the city of Susa shouted and rejoiced. The Jews had light and gladness and joy and honor" (verses 15–16 ESV).

It must be remembered that at this point in the story, the evil edict of Haman was still in effect. There would still be a time when the Jews would be attacked and have to defend themselves. Yet here they were, already celebrating. For now they had a bright light of hope before them because of the decree written by Mordecai and signed by the king!

The Jews felt the tide of events turning their way. They sensed God's hand in their situation. They realized their light was rising. And as they leaned into that rising light, they couldn't help but feel joy, just as when they were in darkness, they were inclined to gloom and sorrow. The Jews were finally anticipating prosperity where for so long they had been brought down by adversity.

So unexpected was the imminent deliverance of God's people that not only were they overcome with gladness at this reprieve, but their honor has returned, replacing the contempt they felt they'd been held in since the proclamation of Haman's edict.

Perhaps this is how you felt when you first came to Christ. You had once been living in the world's darkness, seeing no hope, no real deliverance from the gloom and unhappiness of the material world. But then you experienced the words of Isaiah: "Arise [from spiritual depression to a new life], shine [be radiant with the glory and brilliance of the LORD]; for your light has come, and the glory and brilliance of the LORD has risen upon you" (Isaiah 60:1 AMP). For Jesus Christ, the light of the world, your very salvation, came into your life. Taking to heart His words, "Whoever follows me will not walk in darkness, but will have the light of life" (John 8:12 ESV), you felt His presence, basked in His radiance, and experienced joy flooding you from within.

Of course, just as in the Jews' current situation, you'll encounter some skirmishes yet to fight, happenings that will require courage and fortitude. But now you have the hope needed to wage that war. You can dance with joy because God is in your court. Knowing He will not let you be overtaken gives you confidence to carry on, because you are persuaded that He "who started this great work in you [will] keep at it and bring it to a flourishing finish on the very day Christ Jesus appears" (Philippians 1:6 MSG).

> *The aspirations of good people end in celebration;*
> *the ambitions of bad people crash.*
> PROVERBS 10:28 MSG

> *Thank You, Lord, for Your light. You bring*
> *me joy, courage, and hope. Amen.*

Another Reversal

Their fears remove, their mourning weeds cast by,
They hail with pride the name of Mordecai.

At the news of Mordecai's edict, the Jews' fear of annihilation was removed. They'd earlier prayed for their queen to stand up for them, and she'd done just that and so much more. Now it was time to celebrate. The author of Esther writes, "In every province and every city, wherever the king's command and his law reached, joy and rejoicing took place among the Jews. There was a celebration and a holiday" (Esther 8:17 HCSB). But that wasn't all. For the second part of that verse reads, "And many of the ethnic groups of the land professed themselves to be Jews because fear of the Jews had overcome them."

Imagine. Many who were not Jews, ones who, because of Haman's decree, might have once taken up arms against God's people, were now prostrate before them in an effort to save their own lives! What a turnaround! What an irony! Haman must have been rolling in his grave to see others bow to the race that would not bow to him!

That is the power of God. That is what happens when others recognize that His action behind the scenes brings about the miraculous!

The people of Persia had already witnessed what happened to Haman when he went against God's chosen. They now realized their own lives would be in peril if they tried to harm one hair on the heads of their fellow Jewish citizens. It would be better to join such a group than to go against them. For it was clear that "He who dwells in the shelter of the Most High will remain secure and rest in the shadow of the Almighty [*whose power no enemy can withstand*]" (Psalm 91:1 AMP, emphasis added). Who would dare go up against such a God?

Do you stick with your own group of believers only when things are going well? Or do you allow yourself to drift away when your family of God or part of His church is going through difficulties, hiding until it's safe to come out in the open once again?

God needs people who will stick with Him no matter what is happening in their lives or in the life of His church. God needs people who will say, "He is my refuge and my fortress, my God, in whom I trust [with great confidence, and on whom I rely]!" (Psalm 91:2 AMP), no matter how bleak things look. For only in Him will you find a safe place as well as the courage you need when hardships and heartaches come your way.

Stick with your God. And He will stick with you.

> *Day and night I'll stick with God; I've got*
> *a good thing going and I'm not letting go.*
> PSALM 16:8 MSG

> *Lord, thank You for always being with me.*
> *Because of You, I will never be shaken.*

Superstition versus Providence

Still Zion's foes will gird their armor on;
Obey the scroll of Hammedatha's son:
And rush uncalled, save by the call of hell,
Against the guardian shield of Israel.

The day of Haman's edict had finally arrived. Those who were still foes of God's people were putting their confidence in Haman's casting of lots, which made this day the luckiest for the earthly extermination of the Jews. Meanwhile, the Jews had their faith in another place: the God of heaven. And one another. For they gathered together, knowing there was more strength in a united rather than divided front.

Yet the Jews had an even greater advantage over those who would attack them. While God had filled the Jews with courage, He had filled their enemies with terror.

Faith is an amazing weapon. The Jews, even in the darkness they experienced after Haman's edict had been proclaimed, had continued to trust in God. And because they did so, they could stand firm in their faith, allowing nothing to move them (1 Corinthians 15:58), continually hoping that God would make a way where they could see none.

Perhaps they remembered the words of the psalmist who wrote: "Light, space, zest—that's God! So, with him on my side I'm fearless, afraid of no one and nothing" (Psalm 27:1 msg). Rather than run, they trusted in God alone. It wasn't that they didn't suffer any moments of trepidation, knowing others would be coming to kill them. They just decided to follow the mantra, "When I am afraid, I will trust in You. . . . I will not fear. What can man do to me?" (Psalm

56:3–4 HCSB). In preparation for this day, the Jews most likely dug deep, remembering and arming themselves with God's command to Joshua: "Be strong and courageous! Do not be terrified or dismayed (intimidated), for the LORD your God is with you wherever you go" (Joshua 1:9 AMP).

For God's people knew not to trust in superstition. Not to put any credence in lucky numbers or lucky days. They didn't put their faith in the results of those who practiced such arts (Deuteronomy 18:10–12). They made no god of such things. For they had the one and only true God. He alone would make this day a victory. Haman's ways held no sway over God's people that day.

How about you? Where does your faith lie? In lotteries, lucky days, and lucky numbers? Perhaps you trust in the predictions of fortune-tellers or psychics, horoscopes or palm readers?

Don't allow yourself to be fooled by charlatans. Instead, go to the true source of power and protection, the one and only God who holds your future in His hands.

> *Do not waste time arguing over godless ideas and*
> *old wives' tales. Instead, train yourself to be godly.*
> 1 TIMOTHY 4:7 NLT

Lord, I trust in You, Your Word, and Your Spirit alone.
For You are the source of my courage, my hope, and my life.

Dedicated Deed-Doer

And day by day, by righteous deeds, [Mordecai's] fame
Grows stronger, brighter, till his worthy name
Is loved, and feared, and felt, o'er all the land
Where Ahasuerus holds his wide command.

All the Jews were standing together to defend themselves (in accordance with the edict authored by Mordecai) from those in Persia who were attacking them (in accordance with the edict authored by Haman). But God's people did not stand alone. Other citizens of Persia had, in fear of the Jews' miracle-working God, sided with them, some even converting to Judaism!

Even more amazing, "all the nobles of the provinces, the highest officers, the governors, and the royal officials helped the Jews for fear of Mordecai. For Mordecai had been promoted in the king's palace, and his fame spread throughout all the provinces as he became more and more powerful" (Esther 9:3–4 NLT).

How was it possible that this exiled Jew, the man who had once wailed aloud in the public square dressed in sackcloth and sitting in ashes, was now held in such awe? How was it that the gentle and humble Mordecai was evoking fear in the hearts of the king's men? How was it that he was becoming one of the most famous and powerful men in the empire?

The answer is simple. Mordecai was a dedicated man of God. The only thing that ever made him fear or tremble wasn't the once-powerful Haman but rather God's Word (Psalm 119:161). And it was that Word alone that Mordecai rejoiced in (119:162)—not the honors he was given by the king.

Although Mordecai, when he'd learned of Haman's decree,

had done some loud wailing in the town square, he'd still clung to his abundant peace in God (119:165), for it was that peace, that head-cooling calm, that faith in and love of God's instructions found in His law that kept Mordecai from stumbling, even though the path became rocky. God's Word, His precepts, *His* decrees—and Mordecai's obedience to those decrees—gave Mordecai all the hope he needed to carry on, to keep going, to endure when all seemed lost. Mordecai had been so entrenched in God's Word, had cried out and reached out so long for understanding, and had been so willing to do what God would have him do, that God was able to use him in a mighty way.

When you find yourself faltering, fearing, and fretting, turn to the source of true peace and insight. Open up God's Word. Allow it to penetrate your entire being. Ask God for insight so that you can understand His message. And God will use you in a mighty way.

> *Provide me with the insight that comes only from*
> *your Word. Give my request your personal attention,*
> *rescue me on the terms of your promise.*
> PSALM 119:169–170 MSG

> *I want to understand You and Your Word, Lord.*
> *Show me what You would have me know.*

Esther's Last Request

The day of blood has come. In every land
Where Persia's king extends his wide command,
The scattered Jews consolidate their power.

The battle began on March 7—the day both Haman's and Mordecai's decrees went into effect.

In Shushan, the warriors of Israel killed and destroyed those who would have killed and destroyed them, namely, "500 men, including Parshandatha, Dalphon, Aspatha, Poratha, Adalia, Aridatha, Parmashta, Arisai, Aridai, and Vaizatha" (Esther 9:6–9 HCSB)—who were none other than the "10 sons of Haman son of Hammedatha, the enemy of the Jews" (9:10 HCSB)!

Even though Mordecai's edict entitled the Jews to take the plunder that may have been gleaned from these 500 men (Esther 9:10), they declined to do so. Perhaps this was because the Jews had gone into battle merely to defend their own lives, people, and property, nothing more. Whatever the reason, all the plunder was absorbed by the crown and became part of the king's coffers.

When King Ahasuerus relayed the news of the Jews to Queen Esther, apparently amazed at the power of God's warriors, he said, "If they have done that here, what has happened in the rest of the provinces?" (Esther 9:12 NLT). Then, thinking she might not yet be satisfied and wanting to do anything—or almost anything—to appease not only her but her God, Ahasuerus asked, "But now, what more do you want? It will be granted to you; tell me and I will do it" (Esther 9:12 NLT).

Esther responded with, "If it please the king, give the Jews in Susa permission to do again tomorrow as they have done today, and let the bodies of Haman's ten sons be impaled on a pole" (Esther 9:13 NLT).

And it was done. The corpses of Haman's sons, who had already been speared by the sword, were impaled, most likely on the same contraption their father had built for Mordecai. (The Cambridge Bible commentary notes that the Hebrew text of this passage places the ten names of Haman's sons vertically. "According to Jewish tradition this is to indicate that they were hung one above another on an exceedingly lofty gallows.")* Such a public display would inhibit any other men from conspiring to harm the king and anyone else in his household. The next day, the Jews stood together once more and took the lives of 300 more men of Persia, leaving the plunder for the king.

These events bring to life the words of Psalm 37:34: "Wait for and expect the LORD and keep His way, and He will exalt you to inherit the land; [in the end] when the wicked are cut off, you will see it" (AMP). May you abound with hope knowing the same holds true today.

The LORD rescues the godly. . .rescuing them from the wicked.
PSALM 37:39–40 NLT

Thank You, Lord, for being my refuge, my stronghold, my God!

*Cambridge Bible. Text Courtesy of BibleSupport.com. https://biblehub.com/commentaries/esther/9-7.htm

Victory, Rest, and Rejoicing!

The eternal Shepherd has secured his flock.
They rest again beneath the shadowy rock.
Along the flowing stream in peace they roam,
Though exiled from their long beloved home.

The Jews who banded together in the outlying provinces of the empire killed 75,000 of those who attacked them. But they, like their brothers and sisters in Susa, did not take any of the spoil of their enemies. "This was done throughout the provinces on March 7, and on March 8 they rested, celebrating their victory with a day of feasting and gladness" (Esther 9:17 NLT).

The fighting in Susa lasted from March 7 to March 8, making March 9 their day of rest, feasting, and joy (Esther 9:18). "So to this day, rural Jews living in remote villages celebrate an annual festival and holiday on the appointed day in late winter, when they rejoice and send gifts of food to each other" (Esther 9:19 NLT).

The *Pulpit Commentary* says, "A natural instinct led the Jews, so soon as their triumph was accomplished, to indulge themselves in a day of rest and rejoicing (ver. 17). After toil there is need of repose; and escape from a great danger is followed, almost of necessity, by 'gladness.' "*

As children of God, we too have battles we face every day. But we do not normally take up arms against people. "For we are not fighting against flesh-and-blood enemies, but against evil rulers and authorities of the unseen world, against mighty powers in this dark world, and against evil spirits in the heavenly places" (Ephesians 6:12 NLT). To engage in this type of warfare, we must put on the armor of God and pick up "the sword of the Spirit, which is the word of God" (Ephesians 6:17 NLT). As we do so, we too will find victory.

And after our victories, we too must spend some time resting in God and rejoicing in His protection and power. For if we do not, if we are constantly at the ready, we might, at some point, buckle from exhaustion and stress.

One way to find the regular rest God provides is to immerse yourself in Psalm 23 on a regular basis. There you can remind yourself of the fact that God is your Shepherd. He will make you lie down in those green meadows, beside the still waters, so you can get the restoration you need. As you walk His way, you'll find your spirit growing calm because He is at your side, carrying His rod to protect you and His staff to guide you. Even when you're face-to-face with your enemies, He will be providing for you, reviving you, filling your cup with blessings.

Take a moment today to take a Psalm 23 rest. Bathe yourself in God's words. Then arise with the joy and peace only He can provide.

I'm back home in the house of GOD for the rest of my life.
PSALM 23:6 MSG

Thank You, Lord, for all—including the rest!

*H. D. M. Spence-Jones, *Pulpit Commentary*, https://biblehub.com/commentaries/esther/9-16.htm

The Feast of Purim Established

Oh tune your harps, ye sons of Judah; sing,
In days of light the triumphs of your King.
And as ye keep the Feast of Joy, and raise
To God your hearts in gratitude and praise.

The battles had been waged and God was shown to have brought His people victory! So they raised their voices, hearts, and praises to their God in celebration. For He had, as in times past, given them relief from their enemies.

"Mordecai recorded these events and sent letters to the Jews near and far, throughout all the provinces of King Xerxes, calling on them to celebrate an annual festival on these two days. . .with feasting and gladness and by giving gifts of food to each other and presents to the poor" (Esther 9:20–22 NLT). Each year from then on, God's people would commemorate this time when God turned their sorrow "into gladness and their mourning into joy" (9:22 NLT).

The Jews adopted the custom of annually commemorating these days and called it Purim. Because Haman, "the enemy of the Jews, had plotted to crush and destroy them on the date determined by casting lots (the lots were called *purim*)" (9:24 NLT). Nevertheless, Esther's courage, her risking her life to go before the king, caused Haman's plan to backfire on him. And the annihilation he'd planned for God's children fell upon himself and his sons instead.

"The Festival of Purim—an annual celebration of these days at the appointed time, decreed by both Mordecai the Jew and Queen Esther" (9:31 NLT)—has been celebrated by God's people ever since. F. B. Meyer writes that on the Feast of Purim, the entire book of Esther was read "on the previous evening in the synagogue.

Whenever Haman's name was pronounced, the whole congregation made a terrible noise, and every voice shouted imprecations such as, 'Let his name rot!' "

How fitting that an evil man who wanted nothing more than his own power and name to be respected ended up with exactly the opposite, proving the words of Proverbs 10:7 (ESV): "The memory of the righteous is a blessing, but the name of the wicked will rot."

Yet two other names will continue to be held in honor: Esther and Mordecai. For they allowed God to use them—at the risk of their own lives—to save His people.

When we don't take risks for the Lord, not only do we miss out on what He's doing and where He might be working, but we also end up living a life of regrets. Today, remember that God is on your side. That He can do all things, and no plan of His can be thwarted (Job 42:2). Then step out in faith, and watch Him work a miracle.

> *God gave us a spirit not of fear but of*
> *power and love and self-control.*
> 2 TIMOTHY 1:7 ESV

> *Here I am, Lord. Use me in Your plan,*
> *one that cannot be thwarted.*

Book of Deeds

Recorded in the books of state. . .
Preserved in after times to shape the plan
Of wonders to be wrought in proud Shushan.

When Mordecai uncovered the assassins' plot against Ahasuerus and reported it to Esther, who in turn informed the king himself, Mordecai's actions were recorded in the king's chronicles, his "books of state" (Esther 2:21–23). Later, as God would have it, He worked His wonders by causing the king to be restless one night and to ask for his chronicles to be read to him (6:1–2). And it was that record—the accounting of Mordecai's humble deed—that began to turn Haman's evil against himself.

In the last and shortest chapter of Esther, we read: "His great achievements and the full account of the greatness of Mordecai, whom the king had promoted, are recorded in *The Book of the History of the Kings of Media and Persia*" (10:2 NLT).

The book noted above has since disappeared from history. But the sacred story, the divine account of Esther and Mordecai, is preserved in the Bible. And what an exciting and instructive story it has been and will continue to be.

According to this record, Esther and Mordecai courageously worked together to preserve the lives of God's people, which in turn allowed Jesus to be safely born into the world to preserve our lives as well.

The book of Esther begins by extolling the importance and claims to fame of King Ahasuerus of Persia. It ends by extolling the remarkable wisdom and popularity of the humble and selfless Jew named Mordecai who continued to care for his people and seek *their* peace and prosperity (10:3).

Your name also is written in a book, the Book of Life, where you are "enrolled among the righteous" (Psalm 69:28 ESV). What will it say by your name? What deeds of your life will the chronicler write about you? Psalm 139:16 says, "You saw me before I was born. Every day of my life was recorded in your book. Every moment was laid out before a single day had passed" (NLT). What footnotes will be added to your entry as your life takes shape?

God has given you a set number of days. He knows what you were created to be. Will you, like Esther and Mordecai, allow God to use you in whatever way He sees fit?

Remember, God has your name and number. And He waits for you, longs for you, to walk in His way, to live up to your name in His book, a name that will never be lost to History (His Story).

> *He creates each of us by Christ Jesus to join him*
> *in the work he does, the good work he has gotten*
> *ready for us to do, work we had better be doing.*
> EPHESIANS 2:10 MSG

Lord, thank You for including my name in Your Book of Life.
Please show me how You would have me live this life for You.

God's Continual Care

On earth, from time to time, they feel the rod,
But have their everlasting rest in God.

Although God's name is never once mentioned in the book of Esther, the thought and presence of Him are clearly there, recognized in the miraculous events that took place, as well as their timing.

For it was a period of fasting and prayer to the Unmentioned One that laid the foundation for the providential plot twists amid the pages of Esther's story. And the second-to-last chapter (Esther 9) of the story describes the establishment of the Feast of Purim, a time of praising and celebrating God, which continues amid the Jews to this day.

Throughout the history of God's people, He has shown His continual love and care for them. And this story reveals that the Lord, although seemingly hidden at times, is always there caring for each of us.

In *Bible Readings*, Hannah Whithall Smith writes:

> *The natural heart finds it hard to trust in an*
> *unseen Care-taker; and when Christians wander*
> *away from the Lord and forget Him, they can*
> *hardly believe that He does not forget them. They*
> *talk about being forsaken; and, because their*
> *own love has grown cold, they imagine that His*
> *has also. They judge Him to be altogether such as*
> *themselves in their unfaithfulness, and measure His*
> *truth by their own falseness.**

Yet we know God will never forget us nor stop loving us. For the Bible tells us, "Having [greatly] loved His own who were in the world, He loved them [and continuously loves them with His perfect love] to the end (eternally)" (John 13:1 AMP). We have a Shepherd, a good, true, and loyal Shepherd, who will not abandon us to the wolves. He will not allow us to be stolen away from Him, nor let anyone or anything snatch us out of His hand (John 10:1–30).

We may have times of trouble or hardship. But God's Spirit, His Word, and His presence will never leave our side nor depart from our heart but will be with us continually. If only we would turn to Him, look to Him, seek Him, we will find Him—and much more!

Hebrews 13:5 (AMP) emphatically reminds us that He has said, "I will never [under any circumstances] desert you [nor give you up nor leave you without support, nor will I in any degree leave you helpless], nor will I forsake or let you down or relax My hold on you [assuredly not]!" That's His part. Your part is to believe Him. Begin today!

> *"Can a woman forget her nursing child, that she should have no compassion on the son of her womb? Even these may forget, yet I will not forget you. Behold, I have engraved you on the palms of my hands; your walls are continually before me."*
> ISAIAH 49:15–16 ESV

> *Thank You, Lord, for continually caring for me.*
> *Just as You will never forget me, may I never*
> *forget You as I go about my life from day to day.*

*Hannah Whithall Smith, *Bible Readings* (Wilmore, KY: First Fruits Press, 2018), 273–274.

Becoming Esther

Oh place the fragrant laurel, ever green,
On Esther's brow, the radiant, pious queen;
And in your hearts embalm the name that n'er can die,
The worthy name of faithful, righteous Mordecai.

We've come to the end of Esther's story but just the beginning of our own. All we need is to find our opportunity, the one God has provided for us, within our own sphere. To grasp the opportunity first offered and then to look for and step into the next, continually rising to each occasion God presents.

Perhaps, like Esther, we will not see our opportunity at first. Perhaps we may initially balk at the idea of stepping out of our comfort zone or taking a major risk. We may need to have a Mordecai, one who points out our opportunity to us, helps us see what we cannot see at first. Then when we see our opening, we must seize it. We must, after laying a foundation of prayer for our prospects, perspective, and protection, find the determination to do what we are called to do.

According to God's plan, you are in the perfect place right now. You are the only person in your circle who has the talent to do and be what God has created you to do and be.

Who is your "circle"? Your friend, husband, children, coworkers, boss, teacher, student, father, mother, sister, brother, neighbor, cousin, stranger on the street. Whether you're a queen or maid, mother or daughter, friend or stranger, God has placed you where you are today. He has put this book into your hands. He has a plan for your life—one only you can fulfill. Alexander Whyte writes:

*Only open your eyes, and you will see all around
you our circle set of God, and all dazzling you with
its endless and splendid opportunities, your most
commonplace, most monotonous, most uninterest-
ing, and most everyday circle so shines, if you only
saw it aright. What a magnificent and unparalleled
opportunity—you dare not deny it—is yours, for
your self-control, for the reducing of your pride, for
the extermination of your temper, for your humility
and your patience, for the forgiving of your injuries,
and for hiding your hungry, broken, bleeding heart
with God! . . . Yours is a circle with opportunities in
it that an elect angel might well envy.**

Take God's direction today and step out into your spotlight. No matter how big or small your role, remember He is with you every step of the way. He, who loves you like no other, will not let you falter or misstep. Even if you don't know the entire story or how it will come out in the end, trust Jesus, the author of your faith (Hebrews 12:2).

> *"And who knows whether you have not
> come to the kingdom for such a time as this?"*
> Esther 4:14 esv

Lord, I'm ready to seize the opportunity You provide!

Alexander Whyte, *Bible Characters from the Old and New Testaments* (Grand Rapids, MI: Kregel Publications, 1990), 425.

Scripture Index

OLD TESTAMENT

NEW TESTAMENT

Read Through the
Bible in a Year Plan

Enjoy these pages from
SECRETS OF RUTH
by Patricia Mitchell.

Available at your favorite bookstore
or at www.barbourbooks.com

The Secrets of Ruth

Wherever you go, I will go." These words have graced pledges of lifelong commitment ever since Ruth uttered them nearly three thousand years ago. Yet there's far more in her promise than a heartwarming ideal. Uncover the layers of meaning in these words and you will find that they belong on the lips of everyone who desires a closer, more intimate, and more vibrant relationship with God.

The biblical book of Ruth is a story of family loyalty, spiritual integrity, and romantic love. Its themes of tenderness and devotion, kindness and commitment still resonate today. As you read, you no doubt will recognize many challenges that have touched your own life—grief and loss, unwelcome change and practical necessity. Discover, in addition, inspiring examples of faithfulness applied to real-life decisions, despite the pull of personal preference. In Ruth, see how respect and decency were applied to common business dealings, even though, then as now, self-interest was the norm.

The reflections in *Secrets of Ruth* are based on themes from the book of Ruth. Introduced by a passage from scripture, each reading highlights a recognizable, down-to-earth circumstance that's relevant to our lives today, coupled with God's divine response. See how God uses common events to bring His people closer to Him, and watch how He makes His will known through the faith He plants in the human heart. Celebrate the promise of the Messiah that God fulfilled through Ruth's descendants. Celebrate too His promise of continuing love that He showers on you today.

Famine Strikes

Before Israel was ruled by kings, Elimelech from
the tribe of Ephrath lived in the town of Bethlehem.
His wife was named Naomi, and their two sons were
Mahlon and Chilion. But when their crops failed, they
moved to the country of Moab.

RUTH 1:1–2 CEV

Famine! To this day, storms, drought, infestation, and warfare in parts of the world force growers off their land. Their crops lost, they and everyone in the community dependent on them have no food for the table. If they can, they move to another place and start all over again.

For most of us, however, starvation is a scourge witnessed through the lens of a TV camera. Our lands yield crops, and our market shelves are well stocked with goods of all kinds. Yet we know famine. We experience it when our source of income vanishes because of job loss, a stock market reversal, or a failed business; when the love, affection, and emotional support we depend on disappears with the passing of a loved one; or when our hopes for the future crumble in the wake of a devastating medical diagnosis. Famine forces us to make a move—emotionally, spiritually, and sometimes physically.

It's famine that spurred Elimelech, his wife, and his sons to settle in Moab, a nation east of the Dead Sea. Though necessary, the decision was a painful one. Far from family and friends, these God-fearing Israelites would find themselves living among idol-worshippers with a reputation for decadence and immorality. This certainly was not what the couple had planned and most assuredly not where they had hoped to raise their sons. Yet when they left Bethlehem for this foreign land, God went with them. They took courage in knowing that He is not confined to a place but dwells in the hearts of those who love Him.

Have you ever been compelled to pick up stakes and settle in a new place? Perhaps changes in your health or relationships have turned your plans for the future completely upside down. Maybe a desire to delve deeper into God's purpose for you has started you on a journey toward greater spiritual maturity and deeper understanding. In times like these, "famine" is taking you from known to unknown, from old to new.

Though circumstances can move you away from places and people you love, they can never move you away from God. In Him, you have the strength to continue, an abundance of comfort, and a rich supply of possibilities. He is yours, and you are His wherever you go.

Dear God, thank You for the assurance of Your presence wherever I am. Let loss and dislocation, whether physical or emotional, serve only to move me closer to You, the Source of everything I really need. Help all who suffer famine find their hope, comfort, and abundance in You. Amen.

Choices to Make

The story of Ruth takes place in a time very similar to our own. In the land of Canaan, God's people lived alongside unbelieving tribes. The easygoing, pleasure-seeking, and human-centered ways of the Canaanites drew many Israelites away from God's commandments. Political unrest, culture clashes, and intermittent battles produced social upheaval and the deterioration of authority. Greed and selfishness ran rampant, time-honored values were questioned, the suffering of others was ignored, and lives were given over to frivolous pursuits. Yet then as now, there were those who remained faithful to God.

Elimelech and Naomi held to their faith and the faith of their ancestors. Like us, they were surrounded by many strong influences and may have wondered at times if their pious ways kept them from some of the good things of life. Was it necessary to observe the Sabbath when others of their community rarely attended worship? Were God's guidelines for personal behavior still relevant in this day and age? We can imagine Elimelech speculating if honesty was really the best policy as he watched his cunning neighbors prosper or as Naomi was tempted to join the women gathered around the well exchanging gossip instead of seeing to the needs of her household.

Naomi and Elimelech had choices to make, and so do we. We're not immune from the appeal of going along with what feels comfortable rather than what we know is the right thing to do. Our eyes can't help but observe friends, neighbors, and coworkers living without so much as a nod to God's ways, and we wonder if we're losing out by paying attention to His rules and guidelines. We have a choice: follow God or follow the crowd; lean on Him or rely on our own understanding; give of ourselves to others or take from others for ourselves. We can live as we see fit or as God would have us live.

Your world, your society, and perhaps even members of your own family challenge you to remain faithful to God. As God's child, you might feel like a stranger dwelling in a strange land, even though you've been living in the same place for years. Scorn or ridicule may come your way because of your faith. Each time this happens, your choice matters. It matters to God because He cares about you. It matters to you because standing up for God's ways strengthens your faith. It matters to others because they're influenced by the things you say and do. What choices have you made lately?

Heavenly Father, grant me strength and courage to remain hopeful in a tumultuous world, faithful to Your ways, and helpful to those around me. Through the work of Your Spirit in my heart, let my choices reflect my love for You and my willingness to follow where You lead. Amen.